WOMEN WORLD LEADERS PRESENTS

JOY UNSPEAKABLE
Regardless of Your Circumstances

LILLIAN CUCUZZA
VISIONARY AUTHOR

©2023 Women World Leaders

Published by World Publishing and Productions

P.O. Box 8722
Jupiter, Florida 33468
worldpublishingandproductions.com

All rights reserved. This book is protected under the copyright laws of the United States of America.

ISBN: 978-1-957111-12-4

Library of Congress Control Number: 2023904572

No portion of this book may be reproduced, distributed, or transmitted in any form, including photocopying, recording, or other electronic or mechanical methods, without the written permission of the publisher, excepted in the case of brief quotations embodied in reviews and certain other non-commercial uses permitted by copyright law. Permission granted on request.

For information regarding special discounts for bulk purchases, please contact the publisher:

World Publishing and Productions, LLC

info@worldpublishingandproductions.com

www.worldpublishingandproductions.com

Scripture quotations marked NIV are taken from THE HOLY BIBLE, NEW INTERNATIONAL VERSION®, NIV® Copyright © 1973, 1978, 1984, 2011 by Biblica, Inc.® Used by permission. All rights reserved worldwide

Scripture quotations marked NKJV are taken from the New King James Version®. Copyright © 1982 by Thomas Nelson. Used by permission. All rights reserved.

Scripture quotations marked TPT are from The Passion Translation®. Copyright © 2017, 2018, 2020 by Passion & Fire Ministries, Inc. Used by permission. All rights reserved. ThePassionTranslation.com.

Scripture quotations marked NLT are taken from the *Holy Bible,* New Living Translation, copyright © 1996, 2004, 2015 by Tyndale House Foundation. Used by permission of Tyndale House Publishers, Inc., Carol Stream, Illinois 60188. All rights reserved.

Scripture quotations marked HCSB taken from the Holman Christian Standard Bible®. Copyright © 1999, 2000, 2002, 2003, 2009 by Holman Bible Publishers. Used with permission by Holman Bible Publishers, Nashville, Tennessee. All rights reserved.

Scripture quotations marked CSB have been taken from the Christian Standard Bible®, Copyright © 2017 by Holman Bible Publishers. Used by permission. Christian Standard Bible® and CSB® are federally registered trademarks of Holman Bible Publishers.

Scripture quotations marked BSB are taken from The Holy Bible, Berean Study Bible, BSB. Copyright ©2016, 2020 by Bible Hub. Used by Permission. All Rights Reserved Worldwide.

Scripture quotations marked *ESV® Bible* are taken from *(The Holy Bible, English Standard Version®),* Copyright © 2001 by Crossway, a publishing ministry of Good News Publishers. Used by permission. All rights reserved.

Scripture quotations marked NLV are taken from the *New Life Version,* copyright © 1969 and 2003. Used by permission of Barbour Publishing, Inc., Uhrichsville, Ohio 44683. All rights reserved.

Scripture quotations marked KJV are taken from the King James Version. Public Domain.

Acknowledgments

We raise a hallelujah to our Father God who has made this book possible through the power that works within each of us in an Ephesians 3:20 way.

Joy Unspeakable contributors would like to extend a "very special thank you" to each of the following for their voluntary work of love, sacrificial giving and instrumental prayer support through the production of this book.

Kimberly Hobbs

Julie Jenkins

Kelly Williams Hale

Lisa Hathaway

Kayla Follin

Dave Cucuzza

Michael Jenkins

Ken Hobbs

Women World Leaders Team of "Prayer Warriors"

Table of Contents

Introduction vii

Front Cover Explanation ix

Code Blue, Lillian Cucuzza 1

Wallow or Worship, Lisa Hathaway 17

Journey Through the Darkness, Robin Kirby-Gatto 31

Being Joyful in Every Circumstance, Ethel Hicks 45

Rejoice in Answered Prayer, Catherine La Belle 57

Finding Joy in Sorrow, Mary Simpson 69

Joy in the Surrender, Amanda Jackman 83

What Cancer Can't Do, Robert Thompson 93

Broken Pieces Made Whole, Terry Perches 107

Oil of Joy, Stephanie Winslow 121

Down-in-My-Heart Joy, Elaine Nasworthy 135

Fishing With Bagels, Catching HIS Joy,
  Ruby Tucker 149

Finding Joy Unspeakable in the Midst of a Tragedy,
  Sandra Fincher Porter 161

Joy in Aging, Janet Harllee 179

Joy in the Midst of Loneliness, Nette 191

Why Bother to Pray?, Ann Hall 205

*Joy in God's Faithfulness: The Randy and Pam Barton
  Love Story,* Elizabeth Anne Bridges 219

Joy Restored, Anja Cook 233

My Walk With God Through Cancer,
  Louisa van der Westhuizen 245

Broken Vessel, Connie Ann VanHorn 257

Teachings after each chapter written by:

- Lillian Cucuzza
- Lisa Hathaway
- Kimberly Hobbs

Introduction

Most people have heard or sung "Joy to the World" at Christmas time. But what does "Joy to the World" really mean? How can you have joy when it seems like the wheels are coming off at every turn, and you're holding on for dear life? Or when you are happily sailing through life, and suddenly your world is shattered and crumbling?

Did you know you can be unhappy, even devastated, and still have *Joy Unspeakable: Regardless of Your Circumstances*? There is a huge difference between happiness and joy. It's easy to be happy and positive when everything is going well. But how can you have joy when life takes a turn for the worse?

Everyone experiences storms, heartaches, trials, and tribulations in their life. Right now, you may be entering into a storm, in the middle of one, or coming out of a monsoon or hurricane. Naturally, no one is happy while undergoing storms and trials. But by relying on and seeing God, Christians can endure these tumultuous times with joy, strength, peace, and hope—regardless of the situation.

The authors in this book have suffered tragedies everyone can relate to. They experienced all the heart-wrenching human emotions. They cried out to God, asked why, and then chose to trust Him for guidance and protection. They counted it all joy, recognizing that the troubles in this life are temporary. Despite their hardships, they knew God was in control, and nothing could surprise Him. They admitted their dependence on Jesus, causing their faith and relationship with the Lord to grow even more during those difficult times—because the joy of the Lord was their strength! As you read, we hope that you, too, will recognize that God will carry you through your trials. And what's more, He allows each of us to use our troubles and afflictions to testify to the world of His glory.

In this book, we celebrate that the Lord is our shield, refuge, strength, peace, hope, and JOY. Still, we expect to experience trouble because Jesus told us we would in John 16:33 (NIV), *"I have told you these things, so that in me you may have peace. In this world you will have trouble. But take heart! I have overcome the world."*

Take heart! Jesus has overcome the world! As you journey with us through these chapters and teachings, ask God how He wants these writings to influence you. We have been praying that our God-stories and the scriptures throughout will encourage you immensely, bringing you bright hope for today and tomorrow and joy and strength as you walk through your circumstances.

Front Cover Explanation

The Bible tells us explicitly that rain falls on both the just and the unjust. (Matthew 5:45) Sometimes, our rainstorms may be small and short-lived, like the clouds in the cover photo. But at other times, we may be hit with a hurricane that can last for hours, months, and even years. As we gaze at this photo, it is impossible not to notice the beautiful sunset miraculously backlighting the storm clouds that are attempting to steal center stage. This is significant because even when we walk through a terrific storm, we can trust that on the other side of the clouds, the sun—and the Son—are always shining, providing us with the light we need to persevere and thrive.

Despite the problems the world throws at us, we have the blessing of being able to look beyond our temporary difficulties and fix our gaze on the glowing radiance of the permanent presence of the Son, who never changes. *Jesus Christ is the same yesterday and today and forever.* (Hebrews 13:8 NIV) He is the author and perfecter of our faith. (Hebrews 12:2) Though a storm cloud may pass in front of us, blocking our view of Him, He is always there. Even when the clouds are so thick we can't see His hand, we can surely trust His heart.

In this book, the authors share their stories of walking through their storms by faith, not by sight. They glorify God by sharing their hope and joy, which lie firm and secure in the ever-present Son, even when He seems hidden by the storm. Psalm 46:1 exalts that God *is our refuge and strength, an ever-present help in trouble.* (NIV) As His children, we know He is always there, waiting with open arms.

Now, look back at the cover and notice the reflections in the water. These represent the authors' reflections on the storms they have lived through. Like in the photo, although some memories are dark, it is the bright, hopeful, calming colors that stand out, grabbing our attention. Seeing God's hand can be difficult when we are in the darkest shadow. But when we trust His heart amid the chaos, He sweeps us into His realm of beauty, allowing us to experience His joy and peace beyond all understanding.

The psalmist shares in Psalm 29:11, *The Lord gives strength to His people; the Lord blesses His people with peace.* (NIV) The authors in this book have survived their storms by taking refuge in the shadow of His wings. (Psalm 57:1) And they are all boldly sharing their stories to give God the glory and declare that they couldn't get through this life without trusting the Lord Jesus Christ as their Savior, the Salvation of their souls, and their Refuge. The joy of the Lord is their strength! (Nehemiah 8:10)

May the words in this book speak to your heart, bringing you closer to our Lord and Savior, Jesus Christ, and giving you joy, peace, hope, and strength! All praise, glory, and honor be to God, the giver of all!

Lillian Cucuzza

Lillian Cucuzza resides in Land O' Lakes, Florida. She has been married since 1982 to professional theater organist Dave Cucuzza, whom she met when she bought an organ and lessons from him.

As Regional Vice President of a financial services company, she enjoys coaching people toward financial independence.

Lillian's passions are nature photography and serving God. Her photography accomplishments include First Place at the Florida State Fair in 2020 and 2021, the first two years she competed! In 2021, she was awarded First Place by the Florida Press Association in the Division A Reader-Generated Photo category of Weekly Newspapers for her iconic photo of the Neowise Comet over the Grand Tetons. Lillian's work is regularly published in The Laker/Lutz News, and her photo-art is regularly showcased in art shows around Florida.

Lillian became a best-selling author in 2021 with the Women World Leader's book, *Victories: Claiming Freedom in Christ.*

As a contributor to Women World Leaders' magazine, *Voice of Truth,* she uses her photography and writing talents to glorify and honor God for His beautiful creation.

Lillian's goal in writing this book is to share the gospel, bring hope to a lost and hurting world, bolster your faith, and help you live in joy, no matter how bad things seem. (Romans 15:13)

Please visit, like, and follow Lillian's website www.HisCreationsLLC.com, Facebook and Instagram @HISCreationsLLC. You can also email her at Lillian.HisCreations@gmail.com.

Code Blue

by Lillian Cucuzza

"Code Blue to the Cath Lab" blared urgently over the hospital intercom system as I sat in the waiting room. I looked up from my book, realizing that the "Code Blue" was for my husband, Dave, who was having a heart catheterization procedure done in the Cath Lab! I became extremely concerned because that meant his heart had stopped, and he was dying. There was no one around to comfort and pray with me since I had foolishly declined offers from friends to sit with me during Dave's operation, saying it was a routine procedure.

Instantly I began praying alone. "God, he's in your hands. It is completely up to you. Please guide the doctors and give them wisdom in this emergency, and please bring Dave out alive without complications. In Jesus' name, Amen!"

I sat there for a long moment waiting, and then, realizing I had just given my situation to the greatest physician in all the universe, I went right back to my book. *Do not be anxious about anything, but in every situation, by prayer and petition, with thanksgiving, present your requests to God. And the peace of God, which transcends all understanding, will guard your hearts and your minds in Christ Jesus.* (Philippians 4:6-7 NIV)

How could I be so calm, not worried, and not panic-stricken with fear? Because I chose joy and turned it all over to God, knowing He was in full control. If Dave didn't make it out of the operating room alive, I would certainly miss him, but I knew I would see him again in heaven later. How was I so sure of this? Because Dave and I have both accepted Jesus Christ as our Lord and Savior, and eternity in heaven with God is His promise to us. If Dave's life on earth were to have ended in that room, I was comforted knowing that he would be alive in heaven with Jesus for eternity, with a new disease-free body.

Three hours later, the cardiologist came out and told me that Dave's heart had indeed stopped as they tried to unblock an artery. The medical team used electric shock paddles to bring him back to life, then continued the catheterization without further complications. Praise God! Dave was fine. However, he went on over the years to have many more stent implants, a quadruple bypass, and more surgeries for other issues. Each time, we prayed God would protect Dave and guide the doctors through the event successfully. Thankfully, Dave is still alive, and we are both able to testify of God's goodness, mercy, and grace.

I became a Christian in 1987, five years after my dad died and two years before my mom passed away. I was so excited to share my new-found faith and the gospel message with my mother, who was battling cancer. However, she was in so much pain that she couldn't talk or tolerate noise, and she politely asked me to be quiet. As a result, I never shared the gospel with her. I was devastated when she died, not knowing if she ever put her faith and trust in Jesus Christ alone as her Savior. We never got to have that conversation. I knew she believed in God and was a regular church attender, but I also knew that isn't what it takes to go to heaven. I agonized for months after her death, not knowing if I would ever see her again. It drove me into depression, sucking the life right out of me. Only with the help of God was I able to get through that dark time.

> *The Lord is close to the brokenhearted and saves those who are crushed in spirit.* (Psalm 34:18 NIV)

The enemy saw an opportunity to steal from me and kill and destroy me (John 10:10 NIV) by heaping doubt and fear in my mind. I was depressed, and the doubt and fear were taking me down the path of destruction to a point where I no longer wanted to live.

I finally got the courage to call my oldest sister and ask her if she knew what our mom believed. She assured me our mother had trusted in Jesus Christ alone for her salvation. I was overjoyed and filled with a peace that passed all understanding!

Immediately, the dark cloud of oppression over me lifted, and the sun began to shine. I had an unspeakable joy and hope that I would see my mother again. Now, even though she is absent from the body, I rejoice that she is present with the Lord! And one day, I will be reunited with her for eternity! *You turned my wailing into dancing; you removed my sackcloth and clothed me with joy, that my heart may sing your praises and not be silent. Lord my God, I will praise you forever.* (Psalm 30:11-12 NIV)

I had almost allowed the enemy to win as he tried to steal my joy, peace, hope, and my life. God, in His infinite wisdom, tells us in Jeremiah 29:11, *"For I know the plans I have for you," declares the Lord, "plans to prosper you and not to harm you, plans to give you hope and a future."* (NIV) He has big plans for me. Praise God that I have my joy, peace, hope, and life back.

Because of the unspeakable joy, peace, and hope Dave and I have inside us, we have been able to endure many tragic losses, including the loss of

Dave's mother from the flu in 1992 and his father's suicide in 1995. I was privileged to lead my sister, Louise, into the arms of Jesus on her deathbed during Christmas week in 2015. Knowing I would see her again was the best Christmas present! She lives today in heaven with my mom, in-laws, and my brother, Tony, who passed away in August 2021 from complications due to a brain injury and heart attack.

Recently, my husband Dave was hospitalized four times in five months due to surgeries for coronary artery disease, a heart attack, and bladder cancer. Praise God he survived it all, but for us, *to live is Christ and to die is gain.* (Philippians 1:21 NIV) As Christians, we win whether we live or die! This world is not our home! Jesus and heaven await us for all of eternity!

Though I mourn my relatives' passing from this world and miss their presence greatly, I rejoice because they were all believers and trusted Jesus Christ as their Lord and Savior. They are alive in heaven for eternity with Jesus. Our assurance comes from God's Word: *Brothers and sisters, we do not want you to be uninformed about those who sleep in death, so that you do not grieve like the rest of mankind, who have no hope. For we believe that Jesus died and rose again, and so we believe that God will bring with Jesus those who have fallen asleep in Him.* (1 Thessalonians 4:13-14 NIV)

> *In the hope of eternal life, which God, who does not lie, promised before the beginning of time.* (Titus 1:2 NIV)

> *Now faith is confidence in what we hope for and assurance about what we do not see.* (Hebrews 11:1 NIV)

I know that what the enemy means for evil, God uses for the good of those who love Him. (Genesis 50:20) I have immersed myself in Bible studies, and I knew God was preparing me through these life-and-death experiences for something big, according to His purpose.

In 2018, I was introduced to Women World Leaders (WWL). As a photographer showcasing the majesty of God's creation, I was encouraged in 2020 to use my nature photos and write a column called "A Focus On Him" for WWL's *Voice of Truth* magazine. I had never written anything in my life, so this was completely out of my comfort zone. But God...

In 2021 I was asked to be a chapter author in a WWL book, *Victories: Claiming Freedom in Christ*. All praise, glory, and honor to God that it became a best-seller in multiple categories in less than twelve hours.

Then, in November 2021, my great friend and founder of WWL, Kimberly Hobbs, asked me to pray about being a visionary author for a new book project of my choice. I felt completely out of my league, but I said I would pray about it. For the next four months, as I prayed, every sermon, testimony, and everything happening around me brought the word "Joy" to life! I could not escape it. God was pursuing me with "Joy!" Who was I to say "No"? *For we are God's handiwork, created in Christ Jesus to do good works, which God prepared in advance for us to do.* (Ephesians 2:10 NIV) This book was pre-ordained by God a long time ago. He had it planned in advance. There is joy in just knowing that! But I wasn't born with joy; it has been a journey.

Journey Into Joy

I grew up in a family that attended church regularly. At fourteen years old, I became a lector— reading aloud from the New Testament during church services. I believed there was a God and a heaven, but I did not know God personally. I worried about dying because I did not know if I would qualify for heaven! I felt a heavy weight on my shoulders, feeling that all the church activities I was doing would never be enough. Secretly, my big question was, "How would I know if I had done enough or was good enough to get into heaven?"

I avoided conversations with others about religion. I did not own and never read the Bible, so I did not know whether someone was telling me the truth or just giving me their opinion. I certainly did not want to sound ignorant, so I just avoided those conversations altogether. Maybe this sounds familiar to you.

In 1987, I was on a company business trip to Minnesota. Since my brother-in-law, Tom, and his family lived there, I decided to go a few days early to get to know them better. He was a Bible-teaching pastor, and I knew I could not avoid that dreaded conversation much longer. But I also knew I could trust and learn from him.

Tom picked me up at the airport and wasted no time getting into "the conversation." He asked me two questions: "If you were to die tonight, do you know for certain you are going to heaven?"

"No!" I exclaimed.

His second question was: "If you did die tonight, and you were standing before God at the gates of heaven, and He were to ask you, 'Why should I let you into my heaven?' what would you say?"

I answered, "Well, I've tried to be a good person, do all the right things, go to church and be active in the church, but I don't know if that is good enough!"

Tom handed me a checklist to see what I thought was necessary to get into heaven. The list included things like obeying God's laws, trying to do your best, giving money to the church, doing good deeds, receiving water baptism, and Holy Communion. After I checked off most of the list, he explained that none of these things could help me get to heaven. He told me that there was nothing I could do to earn eternal life. The Bible says there is only one way to enter heaven: Jesus answered, *"I am the way and the truth and the life. No one comes to the Father except through me."* (John 14:6 NIV)

Tom shared that *all have sinned and fall short of the glory of God* (Romans 3:23 NIV), and the payment for sin is death. (Romans 6:23) Feeling queasy, I told Tom I always thought the death penalty was for the worst of criminals, and I've never broken the law!

He asked if I had ever lied to anyone.

"Sure, but they were just little white lies."

He replied that it does not matter how big or small the lie is; God counts it all as sin. He continued to explain that because heaven is a perfect place, nothing impure or imperfect will ever enter it. (Revelation 21:27) If we sin just once in our life, it corrupts and defiles us, making us impure and unable to enter heaven.

So far, it sounded hopeless: we are all sinners, we all deserve to go to hell, heaven is a perfect place, and we are all imperfect. I was getting depressed! All my life, I heard how God is love. Now I was wondering how a loving God could be so cruel and send us to hell for being a sinner.

Then Tom shared the Good News: GOD IS LOVE, and HE LOVES US! *For God so loved the world that He gave His one and only Son, that whoever believes in Him shall not perish but have eternal life.* (John 3:16 NIV) God sent His Son, Jesus Christ, to shed His blood and die on the cross to pay for all our sins, and three days later, He rose from the dead! He died FOR us! By trusting in Jesus Christ as the One who died for our sins, we can have eternal life! That is a loving God!

Nothing we do can make us perfect or sinless. No deeds, charity, contributions to churches, going to church, being baptized, taking Holy Communion, trying to obey God's laws, or any good work can take away our sins or save us. Heaven is a free gift. We do not deserve it, and we cannot earn it. *For it is by grace you have been saved, through faith—and this is not from yourselves, it is the gift of God—not by works, so that no one can boast.* (Ephesians 2:8-9 NIV)

He saved us, not because of righteous things we had done, but because of His mercy. (Titus 3:5 NIV) Mercy means not getting what we deserve—death and separation from God forever (hell) as the penalty for our sins. Grace is getting what we do not deserve—total forgiveness for our sins, making us perfect in God's eyes, and allowing us to spend eternity with Him in heaven. Grace is an acronym for God's Riches At Christ's Expense! Because Jesus paid the ultimate price for our sins by shedding His blood and dying on the cross, the righteous get to partake in God's riches for eternity in heaven! Wow! That is Grace!

But wait. Who are the righteous?

Tom shared with me that the moment I trusted Jesus Christ as my Lord and Savior, my sins would be forgiven, and I would receive God's righteousness (perfection). As Paul says in Romans 10:9, *If you declare with your mouth, "Jesus is Lord," and believe in your heart that God raised Him from the dead, you will be saved.* (NIV) This is the righteousness that allows me to enter heaven! I finally had the answer to my big question, "How would I know if I did enough or was good enough to get into heaven?" It was not because of anything I did. It was because of what Jesus did for me!

I also learned that we can do nothing more to add to the finished work of Christ. It is not "Trust in Jesus Christ as your Savior, plus..." It is putting your trust ONLY in Jesus Christ as your personal Savior, and it is a one-time decision in your life. You can never lose it, nor can you forfeit it. God's unconditional promise is that He will never take it away from you. Jesus said, *"I give them eternal life, and they shall never perish; no one will snatch them out of my hand."* (John 10:28 NIV)

I was so excited to learn this good news that I made the decision right there to trust Jesus Christ as my Lord and Savior! At that very moment, the burden of being good enough to enter heaven was completely lifted off my shoulders! I had (and still have!) joy unspeakable because of Christ in me, the hope of glory! (Colossians 1:27 NIV) This is the joy that equips me to endure so many family tragedies and other crises with peace, strength, and hope.

I pray that you choose joy and the peace of Jesus sooner than later because the alternative—hell— is not a good choice! I cannot make you believe in heaven or hell. You may not believe in them because you cannot see them. But you cannot see the air you breathe either, yet, without it, you would die. Heaven and hell are real!

The choice of spending eternity in heaven with God or in hell, separated from God forever, is yours. I say this with nothing but a heart full of love: please choose wisely, before a *"Code Blue"* happens to you.

If you have not yet trusted Jesus Christ as your Lord and Savior, you can do it right now with a simple prayer from your heart, and He will save you for all eternity.

Dear God, thank you for loving me. I admit that I am a sinner and in need of a Savior. I believe Jesus is the Son of God, He died on the cross as payment for all my sins, was buried and raised from the dead, and is now in heaven. Right now,

I confess Jesus as Lord, and I receive Him as my Savior. Thank you, Jesus, for saving me so that I can live forever with you! Help me to live a life that is pleasing to you, Lord. Amen.

If this is your prayer today, welcome to the family of God! You can have the assurance that your sins are forgiven (past, present, and future). God has said it, and He cannot lie. *I write these things to you who believe in the name of the Son of God so that you may know that you have eternal life.* (1 John 5:13 NIV)

> *May the God of hope fill you with all joy and peace as you trust in Him, so that you may overflow with hope by the power of the Holy Spirit.* (Romans 15:13 NIV)

JOY VERSUS HAPPINESS

In our lives, we all go through good times and bad times and highs and lows. Sometimes we feel we are on the mountaintop, and other times we are in the valley. It is easy to be happy and positive when life is great. But how is it possible to have joy when things are not going so well?

Joy is not the same as happiness. There is a world of difference between happiness and joy.

Happiness is an emotion, a feeling based solely on current favorable circumstances. Our feelings and emotions are fleeting and temporary; they are in a continual state of change. Happiness can be present for a time and then gone in an instant.

Joy is so much different—it is more significant and is not dependent on a situation. Joy is not happiness. Joy is a choice! Joy is a supernatural emotion that remains in the life of a believer, a long-lasting state of being, regardless of your circumstances. It is an attitude of the heart and spirit. Joy is eternal!

Joy is one of the fruits of the Spirit—it is evidenced in our life because the Holy Spirit dwells within us, and we live in His presence. The level of joy we experience in our lives is in direct proportion to how genuinely we abide or live in Him.[1] The writer in Psalm 16:11 says, *You make known to me the path of life; you will fill me with joy in your presence, with eternal pleasure at your right hand.* (NIV)

And finally, joy comes from hope in His Word and is eternal, as revealed in 1 Peter 1:3-9 (TPT):

> *Celebrate with praises the God and Father of our Lord Jesus Christ, who has shown us His extravagant mercy. For His fountain of mercy has given us a new life—we are reborn to experience a living, energetic hope through the resurrection of Jesus Christ from the dead. We are reborn into a perfect inheritance that can never perish, never be defiled, and never diminish. It is promised and preserved forever in the heavenly realm for you!*
>
> *Through our faith, the mighty power of God constantly guards us until our full salvation is ready to be revealed in the last time. May the thought of this cause you to jump for joy, even though lately you've had to put up with the grief of many trials. But these only reveal the sterling core of your faith, which is far more valuable than gold that perishes, for even gold is refined by fire. Your authentic faith will result in even more praise, glory, and honor when Jesus the Anointed One is revealed.*
>
> *You love Him passionately although you have not seen Him, but through believing in Him you are saturated with an ecstatic joy, indescribably sublime and immersed in glory. For you are reaping the harvest of your faith—the full salvation promised you—your soul's victory!*

That is *Joy Unspeakable: Regardless of Your Circumstances!*

If you are a believer in Jesus Christ and have accepted Him as Lord and Savior, you are a Christian and you belong to the Lord. 1 Peter 1:3-9 should bring you great joy!

But if you have not yet asked Jesus Christ to be your Lord and Savior, now is your time! We sincerely pray that the chapters in this book will help you come to a saving knowledge and acceptance of Him as your Lord and Savior so that you, too, may experience *Joy Unspeakable*!

. . . .

[1] Quoted from a sermon on "Joy is a Fruit of the Spirit," by Pastor Kevin Mays, Myrtle Lake Baptist Church, Land O' Lakes, Florida, July 24, 2022.

Lisa Hathaway

Lisa Hathaway is a lover of Jesus that has a passion for the least of these. Her heartbeat is to see those who need a second chance to experience the tangible love of Jesus. She has learned to worship through suffering as a special needs mom, recent breast cancer survivor, and survivor of a tragic car accident within a two-year time span. Suffering has been intertwined in her story, and she wants others to experience the sweetness of God through some of the most difficult things in life, coming alive when others experience the redemptive love of Jesus.

Lisa resides in Lexington, North Carolina, with her amazing husband of 21 years, Everett, and her precious children, Savannah, Andrew, and Luke. She is a bonus mom to Jacob and has a beautiful daughter-in-love, Jessica. Additionally, she is a GiGi to Hunter and Shephard. She loves family and pouring love into others.

Lisa has an MBA and, through the adversities in life, has stepped into God's calling on her life, currently attending Liberty University to pursue her degree in Clinical and Mental Health Counseling. She currently works at The Oaks Therapeutic Community, a Christ-centered counseling and wellness consulting community dedicated to supporting individuals on their journey toward worth and wellness while finding the value God gives each person.

Wallow or Worship

by Lisa Hathaway

I have often wondered why it is easier to feel sorry for ourselves than to be full of joy. Maybe processing life events leads us down a path of negativity, questions, and even sadness. One thing I know for sure is that our attitude is always a choice. We have a choice in how we see life—we choose how we react to circumstances, challenges, and even tragedies.

I was faced with this choice—the choice to wallow or worship. In late February 2020, the world was beginning to shut down due to COVID. It was already a chaotic time as people were frantically processing this virus going around the world. That did not stop life from happening. But I felt like my life was stopping in its tracks. In the last week of February, I got a phone call from my mom telling me the most devastating news. She was diagnosed with a genetic form of lung cancer. My world stopped. How could my mom, my best friend, have lung cancer? How could this amazing woman who goes around the world sharing the gospel of Jesus be diagnosed with this awful disease? But it was true. My body slid down the wall with moans because I had no words. After hours of processing, I felt the hand of God lift my head. I had to get it together.

Then, in March 2020, I was sitting in a meeting at the high school where I taught. We were discussing the option of doing school virtually and what that would look like. I had my phone on vibrate and received a notification on my apple watch from my dad. His words, "I have been diagnosed with bladder cancer," came across my screen. I took a double-take and could not believe what I was reading. Are you kidding me, God? My mom and now my dad, who are divorced and live in different states, both have cancer. I knew this had to be a bad joke, but no, it was all true. I was in a state of depression and disbelief for about three weeks before I realized that was not where I needed to be. I grew up knowing how faithful God is and that He has a plan for all things. But sometimes, when the hard things hit you in the face, His goodness can be hard to see. I am human, and my flesh was rising with questions and disappointments.

After dealing with and walking through the shock of both my parents facing the cancer journey, I began to wonder what that would be like for them. I was still trying to stay focused on my job, my husband, and three children and doing life as normally as possible. Our high school did end up starting virtual classes, giving me a little extra time. Although transitioning to school online was challenging as this was something we had not done before. I was friends with the assistant principal at the school, Holly. We purposely did not show our friendship outwardly at the school, as she was part of the administration and I was a teacher. I didn't want people to think I was "brown-nosing" with the assistant principal. But, outside of school, she and I often talked and shared life.

One day when we did not have a lot going on in school, Holly and I decided to go hiking for a little break and some much-needed fresh air in the age of confinement due to COVID. So on April 28, a beautiful spring day, I pulled up to her apartment, picked her up, and we set off to go on a hike. When we arrived, we decided to do our new burpee challenge before beginning hiking. It was such a fun memory. Around noon we got in my car and left. As we drove back home, she shared with me many personal things—it was a beautiful God moment.

Then everything changed.

I saw a car coming in my direction, swerving all over the road. The next thing I knew, we were hit. The noise was deafening. The impact was sudden. And my world changed in an instant. The airbags deployed, and I looked to my right and saw Holly. I saw her limp body. Her blood was splattered on me. And I screamed her name at the top of my lungs, knowing, at that moment, she was dead.

I do not know how I got out of the car. Strangers came from all over, and I was in complete shock. My body fell to the ground as I kept screaming Holly's name. A stranger shielded me from the blood gushing out of the car. I just kept saying, "Jesus wrap your arms around her, Jesus, wrap your arms around her." I did not know what else to say.

I went to the hospital via ambulance. I was in shock, slowly losing consciousness. I absolutely could not believe what was happening in my life. As I lay in the emergency room, I got a phone call from Holly's dad, who confirmed my worst fear. Holly was dead.

I got home that night from the hospital after tons of tests, severely bruised. My family embraced me, but the shock was so real. The next day, April 29, was my birthday. How could I wake up and celebrate being alive when my friend had just died right before my eyes? This was something my brain could not process. I couldn't quite grasp what had just happened. All the "why's," "hows," and "what ifs" you can imagine came into my head. From that day on, my birthdays have not been the same.

I walked through the next several weeks and months, going to counseling to work through PTSD (post-traumatic stress disorder), learning to drive again, and working to not have panic attacks. I had to realize, over time, the accident wasn't my fault. And I had to learn to focus, with gratitude, on what I had and that I was alive. I started to see God from a different perspective. My healing process was so hard emotionally; I continue to have moments in my life that trigger those feelings I experienced on that awful day. Counseling was and is so good—it has allowed me to walk through these feelings openly so I can continue to heal. God is so faithful. I saw His hand in so many details—it would take forever to write about them all. But He had been there through everything; He never left me. I recalled Isaiah 43:2: *"When you go through deep waters, I will be with you. When you go through rivers of difficulty, you will not drown. When you walk through the fire of oppression, you will not be burned up; the flames will not consume you."* (NLT)

The one-year anniversary of the accident came in 2021, and so did my birthday. I took April 28, 2021, off work to spend with my mom. I had my women's doctor's appointment that day, and then we were going to eat and buy some spring flowers for my deck. It was good to be away from the school as I processed the first anniversary of the accident. A few weeks later, on May 24, 2021, I got a phone call from my OB-GYN doctor. After reviewing my mammogram, they saw a spot on my right breast. I have had cysts and biopsies before, so I was nonchalant about it and didn't let it phase me. That week, I went through a follow-up mammogram and an ultrasound. After the sixth time in the mammogram machine, I knew something was off. Then straight to the ultrasound room I went. I took a deep breath because, deep down, I knew God would be so faithful. The radiologist did the ultrasound herself and said, "We need a biopsy ASAP."

You know, when you get those nudges from God? Well, this was one of those times. But God whispered in my heart, "I've got you, my daughter."

Two days later, I went for the biopsy and then had to wait for the results. On Friday, June 11, 2021, I found out I had Invasive Ductal Carcinoma. Breast cancer. God, really? How could this happen? Now my mom, dad, and I all have cancer. But this time, my perspective of the situation was different because I saw God's faithfulness after the accident, and I knew He would not leave me. "He will walk with me hand in hand," I said to myself.

With my double mastectomy scheduled for August 12, 2021, there were many times I had the option to go down the path of wallowing. I kept asking myself what I did to deserve this. But God is not a God who punishes. He allows things to happen in our lives that we may never understand. I knew I had to quickly get out of my wallowing and turn it into worship. Worship combats all the enemy tries to throw at you. Worship became my lifeline. After my surgery, I had two additional surgeries within six weeks. It was a difficult time, but I felt joy because I knew how faithful God was. God showed up in the nurses, CNAs (certified nursing assistants), and doctors.

After the last surgery, due to an infection, I was in the hospital for five days with two IV antibiotics running through me 24/7 to keep me from becoming septic. That week was my 20th wedding anniversary, and my husband and I spent it in the hospital. Very romantic, I know. The staff decorated my hospital room, gave us cupcakes, and celebrated with us. Only God sees every detail. He does not miss a thing in our lives. I was able to see the goodness of His hand even in a difficult time. Psalm 42:6 says, *When my soul is in the dumps, I rehearse everything I know of you.* (MSG) That is what I did. I rehearsed all that God has done for me, even in the suffering.

There is always a choice. Everything is a choice—both in our hearts and our head. What we choose can change the trajectory of our lives. Choices are sometimes challenging because what is easier in the short term is not always best in the long term. But to me, the choice to wallow or worship is the most important. It can be incredibly easy to wallow through our suffering, dwelling on the negative in each situation. I get it. I tried so hard not to allow myself to go there as I walked through my difficult circumstances. Sometimes human nature takes over, and that is ok. It is ok not to be ok. But we don't need to stay in that place. And I've learned through my trials that wallowing and worshiping cannot exist at the same time. Changing our posture to one of worship during adversity is the only way to seek the face of Jesus. Jesus hears even the moans of our hearts. Sometimes tears fall from my face, and I have no words. That is ok. Jesus catches my tears and holds me so close.

The sweetness of Jesus during the valley is powerful. When I sat on the valley floor with Jesus, it was firm. The Bible says that God is our firm foundation. Sitting in the valley, I knew it was solid. Solid because of the closeness I felt with Jesus. God downloaded a vision in my heart during this season of suffering. I was sitting on the ground in a valley that resembled the valley of the Grand Canyon. I was sitting with my legs crossed, "criss-cross applesauce," and I asked Jesus to sit beside me. He sat down beside me, sitting the same way I was. I kept telling Jesus, "You can hang out with me in the valley, but it is ok if you want to go. I am ok. I know I must get through this."

Jesus looked into my eyes, gently touched my hand, and said, "My precious daughter, I am not ever leaving you. I will be by your side always. I know this season of suffering is hard for you, but I promise you, there is purpose in this pain. I will show you. You just need to trust me."

I sat on the valley floor for a while longer, and we just talked like best friends. I poured out my heart to Jesus and said I would stop asking why these things had happened in my life and look for ways to give Him glory despite the suffering.

Jesus looked at me. With a calm voice, He said, "My daughter, it is time to walk out of this valley. Take my hand, and I will take you to the top of the mountain. The mountain is where you will see things so much clearer than ever before."

I was hesitant, but it was time—time to go to the top with my King and Lord. Jesus never let go of my hand. His grip was full of strength. I know He had been holding me the whole time.

I have learned that joy and sorrow can dance together. Joy is experiencing the peace of God, but even in joy, there are still seasons of sorrow. Just like a slow dance, joy and sorrow ebb and flow in a beautiful fashion. You might not understand the suffering season or the process God is taking you through, but He is God, and He oversees it all: the good and the bad, the joy and the sorrow, and the celebration and the suffering. One thing I know for sure is that God has never changed. He is the same God whether on the mountaintop or in the valley. Through these struggles, I have been refined and redefined. Refining occurs best when we are in the fire. The choice is up to you. You can choose to be changed by the refining fire or to stay the same. I want the refinement process to bear beautiful fruit. If you bypass this process, you bypass the opportunity God has provided for your growth. Growth is a gift we can receive from our suffering, leading us to greater holiness.

God will not waste our suffering. He will always use it for our good. My plan is not always what God intended for my life. He sees the end from the beginning, and I hold tightly to that truth. Proverbs 16:9 states, *The heart of man plans his way, but the Lord establishes his steps.* (ESV) Wow, how grateful I am for that promise. Step by step, my life is orchestrated by God. No matter what the circumstances, I want my steps to be exactly what He wants.

Habakkuk 3:17-19 (NLT) says,

> *Even though the fig trees have no blossoms,*
>   *and there are no grapes on the vines;*
> *even though the olive crop fails,*
>   *and the fields lie empty and barren;*
> *even though the flocks die in the fields,*
>   *and the cattle barns are empty,*
> *yet I will rejoice in the LORD!*
> *I will be joyful in the God of my salvation!*

> *The Sovereign LORD is my strength!*
> *He makes me as surefooted as a deer,*
> *able to tread upon the heights.*

Habakkuk lost everything. Yet he rejoiced in the Lord. When suffering, sorrow, and challenging circumstances take place in your life, what will you do? Will you wallow, or will you worship? Will you raise your hands to Jesus and worship because He is who He says He is? The choice is yours to make. Even if _____, you fill in the blank, there is no better choice but to worship Jesus.

JOY IN THE STORM

As I write this, Hurricane Ian has just caused major devastation in my home state of Florida. With wind gusts up to 155 miles per hour, sustained winds from 80 to 110 miles per hour, storm surges from 12-18 feet, and 10-24 inches of rainfall, many homes and businesses throughout the state suffered catastrophic damage. Some lost everything. Thankfully, our home and community were spared.

My husband and I did not have to evacuate as our home is far enough inland to avoid any storm surge. Still, we were as prepared as we could have been, with plenty of food, water, and other provisions. However, despite their preparations, many people across the state were severely impacted. The fact is, they had no control over the wind, water, and direction of the storm. Sometimes, all we can do in a storm is pray and put our hope and trust in the One who calms the seas with just a spoken word—Jesus!

At the height of Hurricane Ian, as the wind and rain were beginning to unnerve me, I received a text message. I believe God used my friend to send that message to bring me joy amid the storm. The message had only a picture of the Holy Bible with a link to Psalm 107:1, 23-31, which speaks of God's constant love:

> *Give thanks to the LORD, for He is good! His faithful love endures forever... Some went off to sea in ships, plying the trade routes of the world. They, too, observed the LORD's power in action, His*

> *impressive works on the deepest seas. He spoke, and the winds rose, stirring up the waves. Their ships were tossed to the heavens and plunged again to the depths; the sailors cringed in terror. They reeled and staggered like drunkards and were at their wits' end. "LORD, help!" they cried in their trouble, and He saved them from their distress. He calmed the storm to a whisper and stilled the waves. What a blessing was that stillness as He brought them safely into harbor! Let them praise the LORD for His great love and for the wonderful things He has done for them.* (NLT)

As I read that scripture, what joy and peace I immediately felt, knowing God had heard and answered my prayer. He affirmed He was in control, assured me He would never leave me nor forsake me, and showed how He loves me so much that He sent a private text message to prove it! Just wow!

We are all going into a storm, in the middle of a storm, or coming out of a storm. Whether it is financial, relational, medical, job-related, or a literal hurricane, those storms can cause major destruction in our lives. We can prepare as much as possible, but they can still wreak havoc and cause anxiety. The apostle Paul gives the formula for how you can have joy and peace in every storm in your life in Philippians 4:4-7. *Rejoice in the Lord always. I will say it again: Rejoice! Let your gentleness be evident to all. The Lord is near. Do not be anxious about anything, but in every situation, by prayer and petition, with thanksgiving, present your requests to God. And the peace of God, which transcends all understanding, will guard your hearts and your minds in Christ Jesus.* (NIV)

This doesn't mean God will answer every prayer just the way we request. But we can be assured that He *will* answer. We can give all our worries to God by praying about everything and thanking Him for the good, the bad, and the ugly. And even when we can't see His hand, we can trust His heart. And when we do trust His love and protection, He will infuse us with all joy and peace—even in the storm.

. . . .

Robin Kirby-Gatto

Robin Kirby-Gatto is a prolific author with a bachelor's and master's degree in Social Work and a Juris Doctorate. She has been in full-time ministry since 2011, having written many workbooks and books, one of which is *Mindfulness the Mind of Christ*. She longs to see wholeness in the soul, and unpacks scripture, along with the many sciences, in order that people understand the power of God's freedom.

Robin has been an outpatient psychotherapist with adults and children, as well as worked in geriatrics. She has a health and wellness certification, working with individual clients, businesses, and groups on matters dealing with spiritual, mental, emotional, physical, relationships, occupational, and the environment.

Robin has ministered across the United States at churches and conferences, and has done missionary work in the Philippines and Nicaragua.

She and her husband, Rich Gatto, live in Birmingham, Alabama. Robin has two sons, Christopher and Matthew, who are blessed with Christian women, and Chris and his wife have twins.

Journey Through the Darkness

by Robin Kirby-Gatto

The light of truth is made known in the darkest of times, and then there is joy.

Like a huge iron bell on top of a church ringing on the hour, a mother senses times in which her child is on the precipice of suicide. To me, this sixth sense, skillfully engineered within every female by the Creator Himself, navigated my youngest son and me through the darkest time of his life. Understanding our journey requires me to share his beginning.

By 1996 I had two sons—Christopher, my oldest, was five years old, and my youngest, Matthew, a newborn. In October 1997, I became a single mother, and the boys and I traversed through the broken pieces of our lives while remaining in the house. Our emotions, a swamp through which we muddled, alerted us to the fact that we were in desperate need of comfort.

The first Christmas was hard for all three of us. I packed the boys' bags and headed to my parents' place, hoping to bring some normalcy to the new universe we lived in, a broken family trying to find its footing. I could breathe for a moment as warm blankets lay on the floor underneath the Christmas tree. While the boys dozed off, I stared at the lights under which I lay, blessed to know that my two sons, Christopher and Matthew, lay beside me.

My heart, like the Christmas lights, had a twinkle of joy.

Initially, the boys slept with me every night for at least a year. We became the "Three Musketeers." Their two beautiful faces were the reason I woke up each day. I had no clue what I was doing as a single mother other than I needed to be the best version of the love of Christ to those two precious souls. Although I fell short as a parent while journeying through the darkness of the divorce, one thing I was consistent at was taking my boys to church.

Finally, in 2001, I was blessed with marrying Rich Gatto, whom I endearingly call my Italian man. He and I became cohorts in parenting Christopher and Matthew. Initially, becoming a family was difficult; we grappled with finding our way as each person's role was defined. However, in time and with God's help, we matured into a blended family—me, the boys, and an Italian man.

As with raising any child, there were bumps in the road. Christopher, being the oldest, experienced his bumps in the road beginning around 2006. The core Bible verses that got me through Chris's trial were John 1:1-18. Principally dear to my heart was John 1:5. It was like the hem of Christ's garment to which my soul clung.

> *And the light shineth in darkness; and the darkness comprehended it not.* (John 1:5 KJV)

Darkness in Greek means dimness and obscurity, painting the picture of a place replete with fog so dark that one cannot see their hand in front of their face while one trial after another comes upon the soul, individualized like a tailored suit, in which one cannot hide from adversity.

I had known darkness through my own trial as a divorced single mother, but Christopher's struggles were a different battle altogether. Thanks be to God that after five years—on Mother's Day 2011—Christopher's trial ended, and he was filled with the joy of the Lord. Having my prodigal son return home was the best Mother's Day present ever.

In 2009, two years prior to Chris's return home, Matthew began experiencing more of life's difficulties. From 2001 to 2008, Matthew was in public school. While in kindergarten, he was given a series of assessments, one of which was an I.Q. test. Matthew aced it and scored as a genius. Added to his brilliance was a flare for writing. At the age of nine years old, his first poem was published in the Shelby County Literary Journal, titled "Unlocking the Beautiful."

No one knows how life can change,
with very, very mysterious range.
No one can see the beautiful glee,
both in you and me.
But when it comes time to find the key,
then you will unlock the beautiful glee.
- by Matthew Kirby

Little did Matthew know that he had prophesied his journey through the darkness with his first published poem, in which he wrote about unlocking the beautiful glee. According to Merriam-Webster's Dictionary, glee means "exultant high-spirited joy." Nothing could define his precious soul more than this word.

Matthew bounced around like Tigger from *Winnie the Pooh* everywhere he went, with the light of Christ beaming from his face. Many times, as we walked through parking lots or inside of stores, he would do his bouncing stand, lifting his hands to the sky, and shout, "Hallelujah! Praise the Lord!"

In church, he worshipped unashamedly at the altar whenever the music played. From a young age, he prayed for adults, one time standing on a chair with his little hands on the shoulders of a man. Tears flowed down the man's cheeks, undone at the anointing of God that poured out from the soul and spirit of a seven-year-old boy.

With his I.Q. and writing ability, as well as grades, Matthew was placed in the Gifted Resource Class (GRC). GRC is established for future leaders and focuses on using their talents and abilities in diverse areas. He finished elementary and then, in time, went to middle school. It was in middle school that things began to change. The language he was around was worse and bullying was prominent. I'd gone to the principal and other staff regarding the aggressive conditions Matthew endured but didn't get the results I longed for. It was then that I made the decision to send Matthew to a private school.

The Locking of the Beautiful Glee

The core scriptures God gave me at the beginning of Matthew's journey through darkness came from Micah 7.

> *Therefore I will look unto the LORD; I will wait for the God of my salvation: my God will hear me. Rejoice not against me, O mine enemy: when I fall, I shall arise; when I sit in darkness, the LORD shall be a light unto me.* (Micah 7:7-8 KJV)

Matthew and the prophet Micah had commonalities. The prophet was bullied by those around him, and he compared the people to briers and a thornbush. (See Micah 7:4) The briers and thornbush represent the messages of the enemy sent against his soul, as we see with the apostle Paul in 2 Corinthians 12:7-10.

Scripture doesn't say "*if* I sit in darkness," but "*when* I sit in darkness." One thing I learned from God is that one cannot medicate their darkness, the pain and anguish they feel, during the trial. The journey into joy is to wait on God, knowing that He will hear and answer you. He will be a Light in your darkness.

At the private school, sixth grade was still like elementary—Matthew had one teacher and the same classmates for all his classes except art. The teacher was amazing and ensured that all students acted according to the school handbook, treating one another with respect. It was in seventh grade when things took a turn for the worse. He had new teachers for each subject, whom he hoped to impress, and other students that hadn't been in his sixth-grade class, whom he looked forward to knowing.

Matthew began sharing details of how he was being bullied at school. One day, his classmates taunted him after everyone said Allah and our Christian God were the same, and Matthew clarified they weren't the same at all. This was the start of both students and teachers publicly mocking him. One teacher would often speak in a child-like voice to him, trying to imitate Matthew, encouraging the other kids to join in and laugh. In time, other teachers began to treat him poorly, as well.

The reports Matthew gave me aren't worth repeating. It's enough to say it was severe physical, verbal, and emotional abuse. No matter how many pleas I made to the administration, the bullying would continue from both students and staff. Prior to the bullying, Matthew was at the top of all his classes. After the continued bullying, he began to make failing grades. I felt helpless to do something for my son, with continued unanswered and unresolved pleadings. We were in a catch-22 because Matthew didn't want to attend the public school in our district; therefore, the private school he attended was his only option.

I watched this beautiful soul trying to survive in a lion's den. My sixth sense kicked in, and I knew my son needed a way to escape, for which I prayed.

God answered my prayers in 2011 when the school called Rich and me into a meeting. The principal and the other staff began saying things about Matthew's character that weren't true. I addressed the principal and informed him that he had known my son most of his life, to which he responded that Matthew had changed and was now this "bad boy." God provided an escape as they kicked him out of the school, labeling him a bully. But they allowed him to finish the year. I felt as though he had been taken into the mouth of a shark, chewed up, and spit out.

I prayed for God to defend Matthew while finishing the year, and He did. At the sports banquet, his basketball coach said, "Matthew is the most respectful young man I know."

I was relieved for him to be out of that school, but this was just the beginning of what would be another 11 years of intense darkness, as now I had a child with a crushed spirit.

> *The spirit of a man will sustain his infirmity; but a wounded spirit who can bear?* (Proverbs 18:14 KJV)

The word "wounded" in Proverbs 18 means "smitten," which is defined as being struck with a firm blow. Isaiah compares this crushed spirit to dim wicks and bruised reeds in his prophecy of the Son of God, Jesus Christ, who will lovingly handle those with a crushed spirit.

> *A bruised reed shall he not break, and the smoking flax shall he not quench: he shall bring forth judgment unto truth.* (Isaiah 42:3 KJV)

Having been a psychotherapist in adult mental health and with children in permanent long-term care placement, I knew I had a job ahead of me in dealing with Matthew's crushed spirit. But even my professional background couldn't have prepared me for this; there's no diagnosis for a crushed spirit. I have been a psychotherapist for people with schizophrenia, major depression, bipolar disorder, dissociative disorder, personality disorders, and those diagnosed with psychotic episodes. However, this new terrain that I walked was one I'd not known as a professional. And I made it my aim to search out, from the Lord's leading, how best to navigate my son through the trauma and darkness.

I had to find the key that would unlock the beautiful glee.

A person with a crushed spirit has no hope and doesn't want to live. They are suicidal at every turn and have no coping skills. Moreover, the anxiety and fear are real to the soul and lie buried in a valley of trauma, creating a longing to leave life behind. The only reminder that they're alive is the constant pain they feel.

We moved to an area where we were comfortable placing Matthew back into the local public school. This school offered a soothing drink of water to quench his parched soul. He didn't get immediate relief but was out of the environment that had caused him to stay in a chronic stress state, overworking his adrenals. That was an improvement.

Matthew's grades at the new school were better. However, he began to wear long-sleeve shirts to cover his forearms, where he had been cutting himself. I got him into a psychiatrist, beginning years of psychotropics, but nothing seemed to work. He went to counseling at times, but even that couldn't breathe life back into his crushed spirit. At times the emotional pain was so overwhelming that he had to be admitted into inpatient psychiatry.

No words can adequately describe how I felt watching my son wither away in front of my eyes. There were endless nights of prayer and promptings of the Holy Spirit to clean His room. Cleaning his room on one occasion, I found the rusty box cutter he had been using to cut his arms. I cannot tell you how grateful I am for listening to the Lord's prompting. The next night, Holy Spirit woke me up at about 1:00 in the morning with an urgent command to sit on the couch in the den and pray for him. While praying, I heard Matthew's feet on the floor upstairs, pounding through the ceiling over my head. I ran upstairs as fast as I could and found him looking for the box cutter. He said he no longer wanted to live and was looking for it to kill himself. Had I not heeded both of the Lord's promptings to clean his room and get up to pray, I fear it might have been a different outcome that night.

I've been an expert witness in court as well as written on the physiology of stress from both a professional and spiritual aspect. In my studies, I discovered that the greatest trigger for both good and negative emotions is emotional faces. Positive emotional faces bring joy, and negative emotional faces bring fear, triggering the stress response faster than anything else. This is all engineered through the amygdala in the brain. This phenomenon can be seen in scripture where God spoke to Jeremiah that he would make his face strong so that the stares of others wouldn't take him down. (See Jeremiah 1:17-19)

Thus, I began making random happy and silly emotional faces toward Matthew throughout the day and simultaneously ensuring that I didn't show any disappointment when he could not function in school or work. Moreover, when Matthew was in a bad place emotionally due to the lack of coping skills from the bullying, I took time to listen and encourage him. This extra effort required my going to bed later than usual and showing complete unconditional love and encouragement. At times, when he had trouble coping or wanted to die, his anger would come out toward me. I knew it was his pain talking, and I didn't take it personally.

I tell parents in these circumstances to buckle their seatbelts and get ready for a long ride. Always be patient and available, sit and listen when their child needs them, and give them the most loving faces possible.

I couldn't talk about God during this time because Matthew was so angry at Him. It wasn't until years later that God showed me Matthew's perspective—he believed God had brought all the bullying upon him. He thought God didn't love him. I'd never considered that Matthew might have thought God did this to him. But I did know I had to look like Jesus to Matthew through unconditional love and servanthood, not judging him and only giving hope.

For years, Matthew couldn't hold a job or attend college and had problems functioning and doing daily activities.

I often went to bed feeling hopeless and seeing no light at the end of the tunnel, thinking things would never be normal again. It was then that God reminded me that He would visit Matthew in his darkness; I simply had to trust Him. This sweet reminder would give me strength the next day to wake up with joy, believing my son would live one more day.

Before I knew it, it had been twelve years. Each day, I would wake up with the hope that "this would be the day." I realized this journey was about Christ in me, the Hope of Glory!

> *To whom God would make known what is the riches of the glory of this mystery among the Gentiles; which is Christ in you, the hope of glory.* (Colossians 1:27 KJV)

In January 2022, it was like a switch flipped. The Matthew that I had known before the bullying was now back! He had joy again, saying things such as "Amen," and "Praise the Lord." There was a sparkle in his eyes. I found the key to unlocking the glee, and it was Jesus! That was the key!

As we sat on the couch celebrating his journey into the light, Matthew, now 25 years old, held my hand, looked into my eyes, and said, "Mom, when I look at you, I see Jesus."

I just wanted to weep. I didn't realize the whole time I walked through the valley of Matthew's darkness I was becoming the light of Jesus at which he stared.

Scientists have discovered that women who give birth to sons have male DNA in their bodies, especially in the brain. It then dawned on me that the male DNA was that of the baby I had carried in my womb. The sixth sense God gave mothers is the DNA of their child within her brain.[1] With this beautiful gift, a mother can pick up on what her child is enduring. Just wow!

Trusting this great gift of the sixth sense and leaning upon God constantly not only renewed my joy daily in the darkest of times, but it also unlocked the beautiful glee within my son! He entered the high-spirited joy.

If you are walking through a painful trial that seems to never end, know that God is with you every step of the way. He has provided what you need for this moment, and He will continue to provide for each step you take. By holding close to Him, you can experience a deep-seated joy and peace that the world can not comprehend.

[1] https://www.wired.com/2012/09/son-dna-mom-brain/

Joy in His Protection

> *"The God of my strength, in whom I will trust; my shield and the horn of my salvation, my stronghold and my refuge; my Savior, You save me from violence. I will call upon the Lord, who is worthy to be praised; so, shall I be saved from my enemies."* (2 Samuel 22:3-4 NKJV)

God loves us so much that He has given us scriptures to meditate on in His Holy Word that are packed full of great comfort and applicable truth. These scriptures allow pure joy to emerge from underlying actions which threaten to take our joy away. When we have life coming at us from all different directions, God is the One who will shelter us and cover us. We can trust in Him and find joy in His protection as we receive refuge from the trials this life can bring. The entire passage of Psalm 91 is written to show the protection that comes from a God who loves you.

God tells us that He is our strength. When we feel weak and vulnerable, He wants us to lean into Him because He is strong. And He tells us not to be afraid—for He is our protector. With the many troubles we face throughout each day, we need to depend on Him constantly. So it is of great comfort that we can rely on His incredible promises of help, protection, strength, and encouragement that He is always prepared to lavish on us in a split second—just because we are His children.

> *Don't be afraid, for I am with you. Don't be discouraged, for I am your God. I will strengthen you and help you. I will hold you up with my victorious right hand.* (Isaiah 41:10 NLT)

Who else but God would really want to help us when it comes down to the nitty-gritty of protecting us from trouble? God has a personal stake in your life. God is all-powerful, all-knowing, and an all-wise God of the galaxies. He is your Creator; you bring God joy in who you are and what you do. He says that He will be our help when we are in trouble. What a powerful promise He brings in Psalm 46:1, a scripture that says God is *a very present help in trouble.* (KJV) He is right there with you in the present moment. This verse is beyond comforting to me as His daughter, knowing my Father is the mighty protector over every step I take through life. He walks with me. He surrounds my being. My joy exudes from knowing I do not have to go through any place uncovered or unprotected from the enemy's access. God tells me He will NEVER leave me alone. God says He will never leave YOU alone.

You can enter the secret place of God's protection by claiming words of faith. God's Word is full of protection for you to live under every day. Always remember that in Christ, any war on terror raised against you has already been won. There is such tremendous joy in understanding you live in perfect safety, even amid a dangerous world, as you dwell in the secret place of the Highest. He will bring joy in protection—that the world nor the enemy can penetrate. So be confident and trust in Him.

> *This I declare about the Lord: He alone is my refuge, my place of safety; He is my God, and I trust Him.* (Psalm 91:2 NLT)

Ethel Hicks

Ethel has committed herself to a lifetime of Christian service. She has been a Sunday school teacher, a Bible study instructor, and led a women's prison ministry for over 25 years. Ethel is a retired executive administrator who is currently enjoying her season of retirement. Her proudest titles are wife—married 55 years to her beloved Michael, mother—to Tia and Michael, and grandmother to her pride and joy, Dillon.

Ethel spends her time active with her local church, attending various women's Bible studies and daily water aerobics. She also loves spending time with family and friends. Ethel feels blessed to take you on her journey of faith and joy during her thirty years of breast cancer survivorship.

Being Joyful in Every Circumstance

by Ethel Hicks

Have you ever wondered how you would react to devastating news? I always felt prepared to handle anything that came my way. Well, I got my biggest test on August 23, 1992, when I was diagnosed with stage IV metastatic breast cancer. The moment I was diagnosed, the rhythm of my life changed drastically.

The form of cancer that had invaded my body was very aggressive, so I was scheduled for surgery a week later to remove my left breast. When I woke up from the surgery, my doctors said everything had gone well, and they didn't see any cancer had leaked into my lymph nodes, which was a good thing. While I was filled with gratitude that my diseased breast was no longer part of my body, I knew I still had a long road ahead with chemotherapy and reconstructive surgery.

Not many treatment options were available for African American women at that time, so I was asked to volunteer to participate in a clinical trial. Through the trial, I was given experimental drugs and monitored to see which drug protocol I could tolerate. A panel of doctors in another state, who only knew me by the notes in my medical file, orchestrated the trial, directing the treatment provided by my doctor. Although I didn't know anyone else going through what I was, besides my own health, my focus was helping other women face this disease. I hoped my participation could help save someone's life someday, even if my life wasn't spared. I have a daughter and several nieces, and I felt it was my responsibility to help this cause so they would never have to endure what I was going through.

Walking blindly through a life-threatening disease when the doctors no longer know what to do forces you to put all your trust in God and know that He and He alone can carry you through.

The panel of doctors ordered several different drug protocols that made me very ill. Chemotherapy is the process of injecting poison into the body to kill cancer cells, but in the process, many good cells are also destroyed. Over the next six months, my life consisted of doctor appointments and aggressive chemo treatments administered via a port—a device surgically placed under the skin on the right side of my chest. The chemotherapy made me extremely fatigued and nauseous.

After several treatments, I became very sick and was diagnosed with pleurisy, inflammation of the lung's outer lining. The severity of this illness can range from mild to life-threatening. I had a severe case and was in such pain that I didn't think I would live through it. I remember praying and telling the Lord that if it were His will that I die at that time, I would accept it. I called my daughter, who was away in the Air Force, and I began to get my affairs in order. I planned my funeral and signed over a power of attorney for my health decisions to my daughter. After a few weeks, though, the pleurisy started clearing up, and I made a full recovery. Praise God!

God graciously taught me through that experience that even when I was faced with death, I didn't have to be afraid. I could still have His peace, which passes all understanding. (Philippians 4:6-7) I leaned on God in prayer. Having a conversation with the Holy Spirit was my first thought each day. I prayed for strength to go through this valley experience.

I have had a relationship with God since I was nine years old—when I first trusted Him as my Savior and got baptized. I come from a family of faith who supported my decision and helped me learn and increase my own spiritual walk. God already had laid a firm foundation from which I was able to draw; I take no credit of my own. From the beginning, I knew God promised never to leave me or forsake me, having learned this from some of the verses I have memorized over the years in my Bible study classes.

> *"Be strong and courageous. Do not be afraid or terrified...for the Lord your God goes with you; he will never leave you nor forsake you."* (Deuteronomy 31:6 NIV)

> *"The Lord himself goes before you and will be with you; he will never leave you nor forsake you. Do not be afraid; do not be discouraged."* (Deuteronomy 31:8 NIV)

> *"Peace I leave with you; my peace I give you. I do not give to you as the world gives. Do not let your hearts be troubled and do not be afraid."* (John 14:27 NIV)

But, as I walked through this health valley, I realized that my faith was being tested. So I asked God what was in this test for me to learn.

Ironically, I had just conducted a Bible study over the book of James on being a mature Christian. Through God's Word, we learned to count it all joy when we go through trials, knowing that the testing of our faith produces perseverance. (James 1:2-3) Now, I was being put to that test.

I instinctively knew that I would be all right, and I dealt with the pain and sickness by praying every day for enough grace and mercy for each day. That became my daily petition. After a couple of chemotherapy treatments, my hair was thinning and fell out in clumps when I combed through it. I was one of those ladies who went to the hairdresser weekly to keep my hair neatly trimmed, styled, and looking good. So my hairdresser and I devised a plan to cut my hair slowly as it thinned. However, one day I looked in the mirror, and as I combed my hair, a big clump of hair came out. Right then, I decided I didn't want to wake up every day and see hair on my pillow. So, I took out my scissors and began to cut my hair off, and then I took my husband's electric razor and shaved the remaining hair. Then, as I looked at the image in the mirror of my bald head, I felt empowered and thought to myself, "Not bad." Emboldened, I threw on a little make-up and some dangling earrings and revealed my new look. Unfortunately, not only did I lose my hair, but I also lost all my fingernails, toenails, eyebrows, and eyelashes. I didn't know how I would feel about losing my fingernails. I've always had very long, beautiful nails that I kept impeccably manicured. Surprisingly, I just accepted that this was part of the process.

Even after being stripped of all that the world considers outer beauty and appearance, I was still able to count it all joy for even the smallest things. Praising God was the only way to get through the isolation and hard days. Many people didn't understand how I managed to keep a smile and remain upbeat. I knew I was being sustained by the Holy Spirit, who never left me and gave me the strength to continue. Never once was there a time that I thought about blaming God for my circumstance. I never asked, "Why me?" Instead, I always said I couldn't believe He trusted me enough to handle this assignment and told Him I didn't want to let Him down. I wanted God to get all the glory and honor for how He was going to bring me through.

Talking to God before surgery was a matter of thanking Him for the victory that I knew He was going to give me. I always go into prayer praising God for who He is and thanking Him for what He is going to do. I believe with all my heart that He has a plan, giving me the freedom to praise Him for His perfect will, which He will accomplish. (1 Thessalonians 5:18)

It's natural to be hesitant about the unknown, but I was not afraid. I had a perfect peace about what I was going through, knowing God was in control. I have had many trials that have built my faith as I trusted God. With each victory we have in life, our faith grows stronger. We can reflect on what He brought us through to draw strength for the next test. (Isaiah 26:3-4) If you don't have a strong relationship with the Holy Spirit, and this seems strange and hard to believe, I encourage you to spend time nurturing your relationship with Him. The Holy Spirit wants you to come to Him in both good and bad times. He wants you to walk with Him daily, talk to Him in formal and informal prayer, study the Bible, and develop meaningful friendships with other Christians. As you grow in your relationship with Him, you will soon recognize that His peace is the gift He lavishes on you.

After my mastectomy and chemotherapy treatments, I was declared cancer free. I then began the process of reconstruction. Initially, I was in no hurry to get reconstructive surgery. Instead, I wanted to allow my body time to rest, heal, and recover from the vigorous treatments and doctor's appointments. So I opted for a prosthetic breast, which I wore for a little over a year, leading to some funny situations. For example, after I returned to work, trying to regain some normalcy in my life, I arrived at work one morning and went to my desk, realizing I had forgotten to put on my prosthetic breast. I was standing there with lopsided breasts. I just had to laugh. So I called my daughter and asked her to bring me my breast. She dropped it off in a brown paper lunch bag, disguised as my forgotten lunch. That was my new reality.

After a year, I had reconstructive surgery. The plastic surgeon took fat from my stomach to make the breast, so I also received a tummy tuck! Score! After the procedure, I remained in the hospital for an additional two days and was sent home with drains and over 65 stitches across my stomach. For the next several weeks, I had to keep a pillow pressed against my stomach when I coughed or laughed to keep from popping the stitches. The pressure also helped with the pain as my stomach healed.

The Bible is filled with many promises of God that will help you cope with any situation. That's how I learned to deal with the pain and everything I went through. Peace is a byproduct of knowing who God is and what His Word says about what you should do. My relationship with the Holy Spirit had been developing for many years. After I learned that Jesus left the Holy Spirit here to comfort us and guide us in the way we should go, I had the strength to never give up. And I came to a place where I was ready to surrender and be at peace with going home, if that was His will for me. When you realize that you have no fear of dying, it leaves you wide open to accept what God has in store for you.

Now I live in the moment, not worried about what tomorrow may bring. I don't take anything or anyone for granted. I know now God wants me to comfort people with the comfort that He gave me. And I thank Him for trusting me with this trial, knowing that I will praise Him and always keep a joyful attitude and a heart of gratitude for all His many manifold blessings. God has not revealed to me why bad things happen to good people. But He has said that all things will work together for the good of those who love Him, and I trust His Word. (Romans 8:28)

I'm happy God did not agree with me when I said I was ready to go. I would have missed many wonderful blessings. I was able to see my grandson be born and even cut the umbilical cord that released him into the world. He has been my greatest source of pride and joy. I'm able to speak into his life. My husband and I are both retired from our jobs, and for our grandson's first five years, we kept him during the day while his parents worked. I used our time together to plant the seeds of God's Word and truths into him as a foundation. I was his first schoolteacher, and we took him on planned field trips—to petting zoos, waterparks, and fun at the park. I look back on those days as such precious moments in time. Now, my grandson is a senior in high school, and we still treasure a close and unbreakable bond, for which I am truly grateful.

I also learned through this process to allow others to be a blessing to me. I've always been a giver and sometimes find it hard to allow others to give and bless me. Throughout my illness, friends, family, and church family were there for me. At the time of my initial surgery, my husband still had to work, my daughter was in the military, and my son was a freshman in college out of state. However, my husband and I wanted for nothing. I had wonderful friends who took me to my chemotherapy and doctor's appointments. They would wait for hours while I had my treatments and then bring me back home. My friends provided us with meals daily—I didn't cook the entire time I went through this experience. Friends came over and cleaned my house, washed our clothes, kept me company, and prayed with me daily. Allowing others into my home to take care of my household duties because I couldn't was a huge learning experience for me. Looking back, I know God wanted me to learn to let go and realize my body wasn't ready to do these everyday tasks. I had to be still and let others bless me and my family.

I believe I was spared because God had more for me to do, even though I had concluded that my time here was not long. This experience also led me to a women's breast cancer support group called Minority Women With Breast

Cancer United (MWWBCU). I hadn't heard of this group until after I had gone through my treatment. However, I decided to join MWWBCU to help encourage other women going through this process and to be encouraged myself. I enjoyed being a part of this active group as we provided educational seminars with medical guest speakers on various breast cancer treatments and drug protocols. We also provided free mammograms for women and held fundraisers to increase awareness and raise money to continue providing information to the communities.

I'm now a thirty-year-plus cancer survivor. I have lost a lot of younger sisters to breast cancer, but by the grace of God, He has spared me.

Praising God through the pain was such a faith builder. The more I praised, the easier it got to endure all the side effects that came my way. My life has changed. Now I constantly look for things to be grateful for instead of things to complain about. As I've told my kids many times, "Your attitude does determine your outcome." As a survivor, I'm determined to give God all the glory by being joyful in every circumstance. I intentionally look for the lessons God is trying to teach me as I continue to learn and grow in my faith, giving me the joy of encouraging others as I encourage myself, regardless of my circumstance.

Joy in His Healing

We can be confident that healing is for everyone. The word "healed" refers to both spiritual and physical healing. God tells us in His Word that the Lord heals us (Exodus 15:26) and that Jesus bore our sicknesses and carried our pains, removing them from us. (Matthew 8:17) And God also says in His Word that Jesus heals us of sin: *"by His wounds you have been healed."* (1 Peter 2:24 NIV) We can find JOY and strength in these verses.

He heals the brokenhearted and binds up their wounds. (Psalm 147:3 ESV)

We all suffer and struggle with different conditions within our bodies, and it can become easy to lose the joy that once occupied our life when we become afflicted. How do we break free to re-establish the joy of our souls while we are hurting? One way is to become less preoccupied with our physical condition in this world and more concerned with our spiritual condition. Then we can focus our hearts on heaven, where we will no longer have to deal with physical problems. Our true healing, and one we should all be longing for, is when we one day meet our Savior face to face. Oh, the incredible JOY that day will bring when we can see our Savior and our King.

He will wipe every tear from their eyes. There will be no more death or mourning or crying or pain, for the old order of things has passed away. (Revelation 21:4 NIV)

The power of God that destroys the work of sin and the devil, who wreaks havoc in the human body, will one day be demolished forever. But even today,

God, and only God, has the power to miraculously heal—like making the lame walk or, more conventionally, granting wisdom and understanding for healing through the use of medicine. And only God can give us the ability to empathize and show love to others, allowing us to be part of the miracle of healing an emotional wound. There is no doubt that a miracle of healing leads to joy.

But there is also joy in trusting God, whether or not we receive or perceive healing. God heals as He wills, and it is not up to us to question His plans, which are always perfect. There is nothing preventing God from healing one person and not another. God can certainly intervene in whatever manner He sees fit, and we can trust His goodness even when we don't understand it.

The best news about healing is that if you know Jesus as your personal Lord and Savior, you are a healed miracle. Joy Unspeakable should flood your soul every single day and shine brightly for all to see—because you are a child of God! God has made you a new creation in Him. There is extreme joy in this healing—the greatest healing of all.

The Word of God is your refuge and source of endurance when you are overwhelmed with problems and struggles. May you trust in God's healing power and comfort available to you as you seek to know Him more. God's promises are true, and He wants you to remain joyful in Him.

Behold, I will bring to it health and healing, and I will heal them and reveal to them abundance of prosperity and security. (Jeremiah 33:6 ESV)

The Lord sustains him on his sickbed; in his illness you restore him to full health. (Psalm 41:3 ESV)

Oh, the joy that comes from God's healing words of love.

Catherine La Belle

As a Tampa native and a former Miss Florida, Catherine La Belle (also known as Catherine Parks) has returned home after working for 25 years in Hollywood as a film and TV actress. Some of her accomplishments include starring in films such as *Weekend at Bernie's* and *Friday the 13th Part III*. She was also a series regular for the ABC-MTM series *Capital News* and the Disney TV Series *Zorro and Son*. Catherine's full resume, pictures, and bio can be viewed on CatherineLaBelle.tv.

Catherine has also served as chairman for the South Tampa chapter of the international ministry "Stonecroft" and is an active member of The Church @ Myrtle Lake in Land O Lakes, Florida.

Catherine currently runs her own business, Creations By La Belle LLC, and employs individuals with disabilities, helping them find a vocation and purpose in a fun and creative environment. She uses her business website to spread the gospel of Jesus Christ. Please visit www.CreationsbyLaBelle.com for more information.

She is married to the love of her life, William F. Humphries III, who is a Real Estate Lawyer/Entrepreneur. They now live in Lutz, Florida.

Rejoice in Answered Prayer

by Catherine La Belle

Some years ago, while living in Los Angeles, I took a break from working in the movie and television industry. The TV series I had been working on did not get picked up for the next season, and I did not particularly care for the glut of "reality shows" that seemed to be taking over our television programming.

I loved acting with every fiber of my being, and early on, I was blessed with wonderful acting roles. Looking back, I realize that during that time, Jesus' words and promises were very prevalent in my mind and heart. But over the years, God's role in my life became more and more of a distant bell. I gradually drifted off, wandering deeper and deeper into the desert.

As a Christian, I had spent the last ten years floating in and out of love with Jesus, worshipping Him on my terms—that is, when I needed something from Him.

I was recently divorced and was supporting myself while paying high rent in a renovated warehouse in Venice Beach, California. So I needed a job that was flexible enough to allow me to continue to audition for shows and paid well enough to cover my expenses. Acting on film and television is great work, if you can get it, but the real challenge for me was finding regular jobs outside the industry when I was in between shows. My job skills were limited, having focused on a career as a singer and actress since I was fourteen.

So, I took a job on a psychic network, reading tarot cards on the phone for callers from all over the world. I was paid thousands of dollars each month, and, at the time, I thought this was a perfect solution. Besides the great pay, it allowed me the flexibility to work my own hours, and I never had to leave the loft and get in the day-to-day Hollywood hornet's nest of endless, time-consuming traffic.

But I would later discover this was not what God wanted for me.

After several months of this job seemingly going swimmingly, I got a wake-up call. It was not a phone call, mind you, but a deep and disturbing prompting from my Holy Spirit. My Holy Spirit was asking me how my walk with Jesus was going. And what did I see myself doing not only for now but for the remainder of my life?

After much thoughtful consideration, I realized that this job was a far cry from what I had hoped for myself when I first set out for Hollywood.

I began to cry deep sobs. Was this what my life was coming to after all the work I had done, the hope I held onto, and the sacrifice I endured over the last 20 years?

I knew I needed a change but did not know where to begin. I had wandered off from my original plans and abandoned my love for God for so long that I could no longer see my path clearly.

I knelt, and in liquid prayer, I prayed to God to help me.

This is where my miraculous story begins.

A day later or so, a Christian friend called me out of the blue and invited me to join her for Sunday service at her church. I accepted.

The service that Sunday compelled me to clean up my life. The first order on the list of things to do was to immediately drop what I was currently doing for a living and wholeheartedly invite Jesus back into my heart.

I had no savings, no job opportunities, no credit, and no one to borrow money from, and yet God was asking me to abandon my only source of income immediately. "How could this be?" I thought. "Surely our omniscient God knows my financial situation better than anybody." What was I going to do?

That evening, I was reading my Bible, hoping for some help—perhaps a sign or a word that would steer me in the right direction.

What opened to me was the following:

Habakkuk 3:17-19 NIV

> *Though the olive crop fails and the fields produce no food, though there are no sheep in the pen and no cattle in the stalls, yet I will rejoice in the Lord, I will be joyful in my God my Savior. The Sovereign Lord is my strength; He makes my feet like the feet of a deer, He enables me to tread on the heights.*

The footnote in the NIV Study Bible read:

"Habakkuk has learned the lesson of faith, to trust in God's providence regardless of circumstances. He declares that even if God should send suffering and loss, he would still rejoice in God his Savior. One of the strongest affirmations in all scripture of the Bible."

I decided to step out into the void with this same faith; if nothing else, it would be an experiment in learning about God. Immediately I resigned from my position at the psychic network and began looking for a different job. Only this time, I would let Jesus guide me and steer me in the direction He wanted me to go.

What came next was a hard lesson. Our Heavenly Father would bring me back to where He knew I needed to be.

As each day passed, I remained focused on finding a job. I prayed and asked Jesus for help. Weeks passed, then months, and no job was forthcoming.

Every night I would pray to Him. My hungry and weather-beaten soul longed for His love, His guidance, and His help. Then when I would retire for the evening, I would go to my bedroom and search through the scriptures in the Bible. The most frequent messages I would receive were about how many times I had backslid.

The verses that spoke to me the loudest were:

> *And my people are bent to backsliding from me.* (Hosea 11:7 KJV)

> *For our offenses are many in your sight, and our sins testify against us.* (Isaiah 59:12 NIV)

> *Therefore a lion from the forest will attack them… for their rebellion is great.* (Jeremiah 5:6 NIV)

> *I will turn my hand against you; I will thoroughly purge away your dross and remove all your impurities. I will restore your leaders as in days of old, your rulers as at the beginning.* (Isaiah 1:25-26 NIV)

Here I was, sacrificing everything to Him. All I could think of at the time was, "How could He speak so sternly to me? How scary is that?"

I did not understand at the time that God was putting me through the refiner's fire. He was testing my resolve to stay true to Him and reminding me how often I had called on Him in the past and, once my prayers had been answered, how very quickly I waved goodbye and took back my will and ideas—wandering off deep into the desert yet again.

God was using my desperate need for survival to purge and cleanse me.

Let me fast forward to six months later.

Still with no job, I was way behind in my rent, my bills were piling up, and I was so desperate that I decided to take matters into my own hands.

That morning, after having crossed off all the opportunities in the want ads of the business section, I went to the bank and changed my very last bit of money into a roll of quarters so I could buy another paper and find more leads. On the way back, I stopped at a street corner lined with newspaper dispensers. After dispensing my quarters into the coin slot, I lifted the stand cover to retrieve the newspaper, only to have the painful experience of accidentally letting the hard metal cover slam down on my hand. Wrenched in pain, I loosened my grip on the remaining quarters only to have them slide out of the paper casing and roll into the sewer next to me. And as desperate as I was, I was not going in after them!

Well, that was it! My last quarters! And no newspaper.

Despite the severe headwinds I was receiving, I was determined to continue my job search. When I returned to the loft, I pulled out the last newspaper I had thrown in the trash and desperately chose a job as a telemarketer a good distance away—in Burbank. The pay was terrible, and so was the job, but I felt I had no choice. Maybe, I reasoned, God was punishing me for His past grievances against me.

Thankfully, I thought, I had just enough gas in my car to get there and back.

I will never forget what happened next as long as I live.

The temperature in Burbank was a whopping 112 degrees, and the heat waves blurred the horizon. The air conditioning in my car had stopped working years ago—but that was the least of my problems. My car, for some reason, was stalling out at every stop light. The drivers behind me grew more and more impatient, shaking their fists, laying on their horns, and shouting obscenities at me. After many stops and starts, my car finally rolled into the driveway of the destination where my job interview as a telemarketer would take place. I told myself that no matter what the circumstances were, I would get this job.

I was hot, sweaty, and disheveled as I entered the waiting room. I was immediately called into the employer's office for my interview before I even had a chance to check myself in the mirror.

He greeted me quickly as I handed him my resume, then he motioned for me to be seated. Reading halfway down the first page, he looked up at me incredulously, asking, "Do you really want this job?"

Before I gave my brain permission to think up an answer, my body shook, and my voice spoke in an audible and firm tone the answer, "No!!"

Without further ado, he handed me back my resume and ushered me to his office door. As I was leaving, he called out the next applicant's name. My trip back out to the parking lot to find my car was a blur.

As I sat in my car, I remembered the words in Habakkuk 3:17-19, and, without thinking of the most recent situation of my car-stalling odyssey, I turned the key in the ignition. The engine started up without a hitch, and I decided to take the Hollywood freeway home to avoid my car stalling out at the stoplights. What I did not take into consideration was that it was the time of day when the freeway would be in the worst gridlock.

As I rolled up to an endless line of stopped cars, I groaned and despaired that my engine might stop, forcing me to abandon my car on the freeway and walk home. I had no AAA automobile insurance service, no money for any towing service, and I was such a long distance away from any friends or neighbors that calling them to rescue me seemed ridiculous.

I glanced at my Bible sitting next to me on the passenger seat. Out of the most curious desperation, I wondered what the Bible would reveal to me at this moment. I opened my Bible and a page opened before me. It was David rejoicing in answered prayer.

> *Praise be to the Lord, for He has heard my cry for mercy. The Lord is my strength and my shield; my heart trusts in Him, and He helps me. My heart leaps for joy, and with my song I praise Him.*
> (Psalm 28:6-7 NIV)

Then I noticed that while my car was sitting in the worst gridlock imaginable, it was not stalling out. The engine was running smoothly. Well, that was something anyway. At least I would make it home safely. But soon thereafter, my thoughts became focused on the reality that I would be evicted and cast out onto the street if I could not catch up on my rent. Then, as the sun was setting over the western horizon, somehow, a peace came over my soul.

It was dark by the time I got home, and the only light in my loft was the blinking light on my voicemail machine, indicating that I had received a voicemail message. I pushed the rewind and then the play button.

It was a dear friend of mine who had a very successful real estate business in a very prestigious part of town nearby. Beeeeeep!

"Catherine, why don't you come and work for my company? We have an opening for a receptionist while you go into training for the vice president's assistant, and I know you would be a perfect fit. The job is yours if you want it."

I cannot even begin to describe the joy and relief that washed over me. My six months of frantic searching had come to an end in the most victorious way, with the good Lord answering my prayer abundantly, without any help from me!

The best part of this soul-curling odyssey was that the Lord had heard my prayer. I did start that job, and it did lead me to the opportunity I had been praying for—a job that would pay my expenses while I auditioned for acting roles in the TV and Film industry. The job was much better than I had hoped, and in a short three-month period, I was promoted to be the vice president's assistant.

But beyond God working out my circumstances, I cherished that I now had established a newfound conversation and relationship with Him. He not only heard my prayer and answered it, but He helped me to engage in a new understanding of His character. I learned that God is good and in control. I learned of His unending love and guidance for me. Even though I thought God was punishing me, He was chastening me in order to bless me more richly. Oh, there would be other times ahead that I would fall down, but I knew then that God would always be there to pick me back up. I did not deserve it or earn His love and care. And even though I left Him, He never left me.

The most beautiful realization for me was how much God loves us. Despite how many times we take a wrong turn, He is always there, and He is always faithful. He will continue sending us signs, wisdom, and even stalled cars and lost quarters to get us to show us His miraculous ways. Our responsibility is to truly humble ourselves before the majestic, eternal, living God and seek Him with all our hearts. We can trust His leading and His guidance, even when we feel like the struggle is going on for far too long.

God has a purpose for everything we go through. As His children, we can rejoice in all circumstances, knowing our loving God is there, listening and responding to all our prayers and seeing all our pain and trials. I rejoiced in His answered prayer and felt joy unspeakable in my newfound peace! I had found my connection to God and my reunion with Him after so many years of feeling lost.

God promises to answer our prayers if we just keep walking toward Him. One day we will be able to look back and see His perfectly ordained path—until then, we can walk in joy knowing that the day will come when we will dwell in His house in heaven for eternity!

Joy in His Provision

Over and over throughout the Bible, scriptures refer to God's provision. One scripture alone states it all so clearly. By abiding in the words of this verse, we can remain joyful in God's provision—even when we have doubts that our needs will be met: *My God will supply all your needs according to His riches in glory in Christ Jesus.* (Philippians 4:19 KJV)

God has everything good in mind for those He loves. He would never give us what He knows would harm us. He is our Father in heaven, and He refers to us as His children. Would any good parent ever not provide for their child? Yet the difference between an earthly parent and our Heavenly Father is that God knows our hearts and can differentiate between our needs and wants. It brings me exuberant joy knowing I can shift my focus from what the world says I need and resolve to accept what God says I need, trusting He knows my heart. And what's more, God sees my every need before I even ask. When we learn to trust God's wisdom in the difference between our needs and wants, we can see life in a whole new light. We can trust God to provide what is best. We can ask Him for what we think we need while remaining confident He will provide what He knows we need. Only God can see our lives completely—from the beginning to the end and everything in between. We can be joyful knowing His provisions are infinite and perfect.

God's goodness, guidance, and care will do more for us than we could ever imagine or achieve on our own. God is always providing a way for us to develop a closer, more intimate, conversational, and obedient relationship with Him so that we can lead others to the care He provides for us.

> *You, LORD, are my shepherd. I will never be in need.* (Psalm 23:1 CEV)

God wants a relationship with you—and you can verbalize your needs to Him, even though He already knows them. He will not withhold anything from you if you walk closely and obediently with Him.

> *For the LORD God is our sun and our shield; the LORD bestows favor and honor; no good thing does he withhold from those whose walk is blameless.* (Psalm 84:11 NIV)

Yes, God is our provider in so many ways, in every way. We may limit our thoughts of God's provision to those of food and clothing, homes, or jobs, but we should cherish and treasure our assurance of His love for us even more. God's love is the greatest provision of all. He loved us even before we were conceived. What a joy to know that God has been involved in our lives, providing us with such love from the very start! His love for us equips us to be the best we can be. He gives us everything we need, including the sun that rises, the wind that blows, and the rain that refreshes. He provides it all. We can all marvel at the unending joy of His provision!

Mary Simpson

Mary Simpson is a native of Ohio, where her father was a pastor for 30 years. She is one of twelve children—from which she learned the joys of having brothers and sisters. Mary met her husband, Jerry, in Chicago, Illinois, in 1971 while she was working as a nurse at Children's Hospital. After marrying in 1972, they moved to Fort Lauderdale, Florida, with his job relocation.

After her two children began school, Mary went back into nursing part-time, working for hospitals and various doctor's offices.

After 32 years in Fort Lauderdale, Jerry got an early retirement package, and they relocated to the Dallas, Texas, area, where their two children had settled in with their jobs and families. There they enjoyed retirement with part-time jobs to allow for travel. God graced them with the blessings of two grandchildren, bringing much pleasure in growing older.

Finding Joy in Sorrow

by Mary Simpson

Finding joy in sorrow may sound impossible, but I write to you today from a personal standpoint of *looking* for joy in the midst of my own sorrow. My journey has not been perfect, but through it, I continue to learn and grow. And it is my prayer that by reading my story, you will learn and grow, too.

To begin my story, I must go back to January 2020, when my youngest sister, Beth, had a brain injury due to a bicycle accident. She was in the hospital for five months. During that time, the United States experienced the introduction of COVID, and hospitals and rehabilitation centers closed down to visitors. As her family, we had to rely on reports from doctors and nurses regarding Beth's progress. Due to her brain injury, she suffered severe loss of blood and had five aneurysms, damaging her reasoning ability.

While she was in the hospital, I began sending my sister encouraging cards and letters every week. I came to understand she could not read at that time or even comprehend most of the cards and letters. But even though she could not read them, I continued sending them to remind her that God, our great physician, was taking care of her.

Fast forward to July 2021. Beth had gained back 85% of her physical health, and all of us siblings and her family planned a family reunion to celebrate her miraculous recovery. Our theme was "To God Be The Glory." Plans began to take shape for 50 family members to gather in our hometown in Ohio. Our home church has a campground where we've held most of our family reunions, so that was the logical place for the celebration. We were going to use Sunday morning as our family sharing time, focusing on the lessons we learned from God as we were in the "waiting room" for 18 months, anticipating Beth's recovery.

For this time of sharing, God directed me to share about Laura Story's book *When God Doesn't Fix It*. Even as we all gloried in the blessings of God giving Beth physical healing, we would still need to recognize the effects her brain injury had on her reasoning ability. I planned to finish my remarks by saying, "When things turn out the way we want them to, we always say God is good. But is He still good when things don't turn out the way we prayed or wanted them to?"

Little did I know that God would soon use that phrase to test my faith.

My husband, Jerry, and I made plans to travel from Texas to Ohio for the reunion, but God alone orchestrated our trip. We took our two grandkids with us as their parents could not attend. The kids loved to go camping in our 5th wheel, and we loved taking them with us whenever we got the chance. We stopped in Kentucky to visit the Ark Encounter and the Creation Museum, which they thoroughly enjoyed. Then we headed on to Ohio to spend a couple of days with Jerry's siblings and their grandchildren, enjoying two days of wonderful family time with them. Those were definitely God's steps in our plans. Our next stop was my hometown, where we reveled in an amazing weekend and one of the best family reunions we have ever had—another one of God's steps in our plans.

Jerry has always loved amusement parks; he would seek out the wildest roller coasters to give a try. This same adventurous spirit led him to love zip-lining.

Prior to our trip, he discovered that the campground we would be staying at had a zip line going over a small lake, and he had looked forward to this adventure for months. He was like a little boy, telling all his buddies that he was going zip-lining. And he did! Not just once but a least six times! Yes, he was like a little boy with a new adventure. That was his thrill of the weekend, and he finished it off by filling 100 water balloons for all the younger children to enjoy a water balloon fight—another one of God's steps in our plans.

Leaving the family reunion, we were all on a mountaintop, carrying wonderful memories and blessings from God. However, Jerry and I began to feel unwell on our way home. We attributed our symptoms to being on the go for a week, doing activities that people of our age don't normally do, or allergies that had been exacerbated by being in a different area of the country. Little did we know the next steps God had for us, despite our plans.

I have been using the words "plans" and "God's steps" in this recounting of our trip to Ohio for a particular reason. When Jerry retired and we started traveling, we chose Proverbs 16:9 as our retirement verse: *A man's heart plans his way, but the LORD directs his steps.* (NKJV) In fact, we had that printed on our 5th wheel spare tire cover as a reminder when we took our trips away from home. Many times, we were faced with unplanned situations, and this verse became a reality in our travels.

God sent His angels to watch over us and to get us home safely. *For He shall give His angels charge over you, to keep you in all your ways.* (Psalm 91:11 NKJV) Jerry never mentioned how sick he was beginning to feel, and I was in a brain fog while keeping watch over the grandkids. After getting home and spending a day in bed, Jerry finally said he thought he needed to go to the hospital.

We both tested positive for COVID. And Jerry was admitted to the hospital with COVID pneumonia.

At that time, our church was studying the book *The Strength You Need* by Robert Morgan. When I began to feel better, I began to read it. Every day, the Bible verses gave me the God-given strength I needed to pray and pray and pray for Jerry's recovery. I never lost faith that God was not going to answer my prayer.

He did. But not here on earth. God healed my Jerry in heaven.

I wrestled with God's answer for many weeks. I know God's ways are not our ways, but I am human. I had prayed boldly Hebrews 4:16, *So let us come boldly to the throne of our gracious God.* (NLT)

One day when I was talking to the Lord, I just said, "Lord, I know You could have healed Jerry on earth, so why did you not do that?"

In His quiet voice, I heard God say, "Yes, Mary, I could have, but I knew what was ahead for you and Jerry if I healed him on earth, so in My mercy and love, I took him in My arms and healed him in heaven."

Such peace came over me, and I have never questioned that again. Just recently, I read Hebrews 4:16 in my quiet time with the Lord, and although I had memorized that whole verse, the light bulb came on, illuminating the meaning of the second part of the verse, *There we will receive His mercy, and we will find grace to help us when we need it the most.* (NLT) WOW! And I needed His help the most as I turned a new chapter of my life.

I had to face the question I asked at my family reunion: "Is God still good when things didn't turn out the way I wanted them to?"

This question is a very soul-searching one when we are faced with a huge test of trusting God's hand.

Yet even in pain and sorrow, I found God's goodness to me.

1) He promised to always be with me.
   He will not leave you nor forsake you. (Deuteronomy 31:6 NKJV)

2) He promised that all things would change, but Jesus will never change.
   Jesus Christ is the same yesterday, today, and forever. (Hebrews 13:8 NKJV)

3) He assured me that He is my comforter.
   The LORD is near to those who have a broken heart. (Psalm 34:18 NKJV)

4) He promises to meet my every need.
   And my God shall supply all your needs according to His riches in glory by Christ Jesus. (Philippians 4:19 NKJV)

5) He sent His Son to be our sacrifice for sins if we accept His gift of salvation.
   For God presented Jesus as the sacrifice for sin. (Romans 3:25 NLT)
   God saved you by His grace when you believed. (Ephesians 2:8 NLT)

6) He has given us, in Christ, a residence in heaven when we die.
   When everything is ready, I will come and get you, so that you will always be with me where I am. (John 14:3 NLT)

Yes! God is good even in the most trying of times. However, I was struggling with being *thankful and joyful*—as the Bible tells us to be—when my life was turned upside down after losing my faithful husband of 49 years. I grew up as a preacher's kid, learning the scriptures since childhood, but I realized that head knowledge of those two words, thankful and joyful, didn't mean anything until I was put to the test.

Then, even as I battled through my grief, I was asked to pray about writing in this book—a book about joy. I thought what an impossible task that would be as I was struggling with being thankful, let alone joyful. But then I began to understand this was an assignment from God. He was leading me to search the Scriptures and learn from Him. And what I found is that God is okay with us wrestling to discover His answers, for through wrestling comes rest.

One of the most impactful things I learned is that thanksgiving and joy go hand in hand. Joy is a fruit of the Spirit within me, whereas thanksgiving is my attitude.

> *Let us come to Him with thanksgiving.* (Psalm 95:2 NLT)

> *And always be thankful.* (Colossians 3:15 NLT)

> *With thanksgiving, let your requests be made known to God.* (Philippians 4:6 NKJV)

Thankful, thankful, thankful! But I am NOT thankful that God separated my husband and me through death, so how can I be thankful?

As I prayed and spent quiet time with the Lord, He began to show me the right attitude of being thankful.

- Be thankful for the man He gave me and the wonderful 49 years living our life together.
- Be thankful that he did not suffer a long illness.
- Be thankful for the precious ten days I spent with him in the hospital before he was taken to the intensive care unit. That was definitely a God thing!
- Be thankful for the peace that God promises in times like this.
- Be thankful for Christian friends and family who genuinely hold me up in prayer.

And so on. Yes, I have many, many things to be thankful for. And yet it's okay to go through the grieving process. Being thankful is a daily attitude process.

Now that I'd worked through the word thanksgiving, I had to tackle the word joy—which was my real assignment if I were to write this chapter. As I mentioned, thanksgiving and joy go hand in hand, so one is void without the other. Still, joy is a much bigger word when facing life without my security, my stable husband. How can I find joy when my life has been permanently turned upside down? Where is joy when God gives you the hardest test of faith in trusting Him?

Spending time with the Lord is the only way I have learned what it means to have joy in my life. I have always found Christian authors, whom God has led in their lives, to help me when I face situations that are out of my understanding. This is certainly one of those times. I began reading a book I found in my office that I had bought years ago by Elizabeth George, *Finding God's Path Through Your Trials,* in which she uses James 1 as her study. Through this book, the Lord gave me a new understanding of His purpose for going through this difficult time in my life. Joy is allowing my Creator to cultivate the fruit of joy given to me from the Holy Spirit's work in my life. (Galatians 5:22) It is taking the unwanted circumstances and establishing His purpose in being conformed to His Son's image. *And we know that all things work together for good to those who love God, to those who are the called according to His purpose. For whom He foreknew, He also predestined to be conformed to the image of His Son, that He might be the firstborn among many brethren.* (Romans 8:28-29 NKJV)

Hebrews 12:2 says that Jesus endured the cross with joy. Why? Because He knew what was awaiting Him when He finished the work His Father had sent Him to do. Through His suffering and death, Jesus gave eternal life—a place with Him in glory—to all who call upon His name.

Joy to me is finding myself on the path He has prepared for me and knowing it is now just God and me traveling on our adventure together. This is a huge step in trust. God's promise for me is in Psalm 32:8, *The Lord says, "I will guide you along the best pathway for your life, I will advise you and watch over you."* (NLT) Now comes my part of trusting and obeying. One of the paths He has taken me on in the past two years is reaching out to other women who have lost their husbands for a monthly time of encouragement. We understand and lean on each other, and yet we need God's encouragement to focus on Him and not our circumstances.

In closing, I must say I am still human, and I am still grieving. There are days when Satan attacks me. However, I push forward with God as my emotional and physical strength. For in Him is my joy, creating in me a thankful attitude and a joyful heart toward The One who knows me best.

Just as God gave the Israelites daily manna in the wilderness (Exodus 16:4), He gives me only enough strength for each day. Each morning, I acknowledge my weakness so He can infuse me with His power. 2 Corinthians 12:9

reminds me, *"My grace is sufficient for you, for My strength is made perfect in weakness."* (NKJV) Each morning, *His mercies are new. Great is Your faithfulness.* (Lamentations 3:23 NKJV)

I hope to look back someday on this adventure God is taking me and say with thanksgiving and, yes, JOY that Jesus led me all the way. If you let Him, He will lead you, too.

Joy in the Mourning

One of the most heart-wrenching things to experience is the loss of a loved one. Whether they died unexpectedly or from a long illness, it still hurts and leaves a huge hole in our hearts as we mourn their absence. It's okay to cry and grieve! We are human. And there is no set timeline for the grieving process—everyone's mourning period is different.

So how is it possible to have joy in the mourning? Joy is not an emotion. It is a choice, an attitude of the heart, and it is supernatural. It is the opposite of grieving—it is comforting. It is trusting God's heart when you can't see His hand and knowing He has it all under control.

When Jesus died on the cross, His followers mourned. Their mourning turned to joy three days later when He rose from the grave to defeat death and offer eternal life to all who believe in Him.

We have joy because we have the promise of eternal life! *For God so loved the world that He gave His one and only Son, that whoever believes in Him shall not perish but have eternal life.* (John 3:16 NIV)

Jesus lives and sits at the right hand of the Father in heaven. He is preparing a place for us. Jesus told us, *"Do not let your hearts be troubled. You believe in God; believe also in Me. My Father's house has many rooms; if that were not so, would I have told you that I am going there to prepare a place for you? And if I go and prepare a place for you, I will come back and take you to be with Me that you also may be where I am."* (John 14:1-3 NIV)

Paul reassures our hope in 1 Thessalonians 4:13-14, *Brothers and sisters, we do not want you to be uninformed about those who sleep in death, so that you do not grieve like the rest of mankind, who have no hope. For we believe that Jesus died and rose again, and so we believe that God will bring with Jesus those who have fallen asleep in him.* (NIV)

That is *Joy Unspeakable!*

Jesus sent Holy Spirit to be the Comforter in the hearts of believers. We don't have the human strength to overcome grief and mourning. But if we have Holy Spirit living in us, then the joy of the Lord is our strength. (Nehemiah 8:10)

When someone physically dies, they are absent from the body, but they are immediately present with Jesus in heaven if they accepted Him as their Savior before they died. If a loved one died as a believer, then you can rest assured they are in heaven right now, more alive than ever. *In the hope of eternal life, which God, who does not lie, promised before the beginning of time.* (Titus 1:2 NIV)

But what if someone died and you are not sure if they were a believer? We have the hope of heaven. Unbeknownst to you, that person may have asked Jesus for forgiveness and accepted Him as their Savior in their last breath, even if they were unconscious. Studies have shown that some people in comas picked up and processed sounds even though they couldn't respond, meaning it is possible they could hear and accept what was spoken to them. Only God knows our hearts and our response to Him. This is where trusting God and the hope of heaven for our dying loved ones come in. If they did hear and accept, they are alive in heaven with Jesus forever. We will be reunited with our loved ones!

Of course, no one knows when their time is up; therefore, we cannot afford to wait until the last minute to ask Jesus into our heart. After all, we may not get another opportunity.

My sister had not accepted Jesus as her Savior until she was on her deathbed. She was unable to speak but communicated by blinking her eyes. I was privileged to share the gospel message with her. Even though she could not verbally ask Jesus into her heart, she blinked a huge "YES" that she believed and wanted Jesus to be her Lord and Savior. I left that hospital with the assurance that when she closed her eyes for the last time here on earth, she would open them in the arms of Jesus in heaven in a split second! She died four days later on Christmas Eve. Although I miss her, I rejoice with the angels in a supernatural way that has carried me ever since because I know she is more alive than ever, in a new body, walking the streets of gold, and I will see her again when I pass into eternity.

Jesus tells us in John 16:22, *"Now is your time of grief, but I will see you again and you will rejoice, and no one will take away your joy."* (NIV)

Because He lives, I have Joy in the Mourning!

. . . .

Amanda Jackman

Amanda Jackman is from the small town of Imlay City, Michigan. She and her husband, Brad, have four children under the age of six (Bradley-6, Juliet-5, Walter-4, and Arthur-2). She has a Paralegal Studies degree and enjoys reading and writing. She loves the busy life of being a wife and mother of four and mostly stays at home with her children. She also contributes in business with her husband and mother.

Amanda is a freelance writer for her local newspaper, president of a scholarship foundation, founder of a local women's networking group, and a contributing author for Women World Leaders' *Voice of Truth* magazine with the column "Reheated Coffee."

Joy in the Surrender
by Amanda Jackman

Every woman who has ever miscarried understands the grief and loss associated with losing a child. Each child, even when not "viable" to live on his own, was created by our heavenly Father. Even the children whose lungs never have the opportunity to breathe oxygen are given life purposefully. They are an integral part of our human family, connected by heartstrings to their mother for eternity. And the well of a mother's love runs deep— regardless of the length of the child's life. I know. When I step into heaven's glory, some of my own children will be there to greet me for the first time. But for now, how do I walk in joy despite my heartbreak?

Stigma and statistics have made women suffer in silence for years. One in four women experience miscarriage, and one in one hundred have experienced recurring pregnancy loss. Miscarriage occurs so frequently that often women don't even announce their pregnancy until they are out of their first trimester.

Yet, talking about miscarriage can make people uncomfortable. They say things like, "At least you're still young." "At least you know you can get pregnant," "At least it was early." Or, "God needed your baby more than you did. They are in a better place."

These are all phrases I've been on the receiving end of. But from the perspective of the woman who miscarried, it can feel as though these well-intentioned friends or family members negate your loss simply because your child never took a breath. Loss is loss. Grief is grief.

After giving birth to four beautiful children in just over four years, I felt like I had beat the odds of miscarriage. My husband and I didn't know if we wanted more children—having four under the age of four is pretty hectic and overwhelming. Then I saw the positive pregnancy test for baby number five. This would be five children in five years for us! What were we thinking?! We were thinking that every baby is a blessing, a perfect gift from God. *Every good and perfect gift is from above.* (James 1:17 NIV)

Two weeks later, I was on my way home when I felt a rush of blood. I knew that meant my baby was gone. The hospital later that evening confirmed that I had lost the pregnancy at six weeks. God, how could this be? We wanted this baby. This was something that we had never experienced before, and we were a little bit shocked.

Then, three months later, we lost a second pregnancy. This pregnancy was hard because, from the moment I saw the positive test, I wondered when I would lose this baby. That was a spiritual attack. Fear can become so consuming; it can cripple you. It did for me. My fear became a reality.

When I found myself pregnant again two months later, I couldn't even be happy because I was paralyzed with foreboding, believing that if I became attached to the baby, I would lose it too. And we did.

After having three consecutive miscarriages, a doctor will perform an intensive check on the grieving woman's blood and hormone levels. I went through this process, but twelve tests later, my doctor couldn't find anything medically "wrong" with me that would cause me to lose three pregnancies. It was a lonely place with no real answers. So I went to the Lord in prayer, so specifically about pregnancy loss.

Seeking Jesus, I received a clear answer.

If I had never experienced a miscarriage, I would never have had the opportunity to minister and comfort other women as they experience this type of loss. I wouldn't be able to understand the depths of their pain and grief. God allowed me to experience that suffering so that, later, I could be a comfort to one of my friends who had an early loss. My friend was lost and confused, and I was able to be there for her—because I understood what she was going through.

When I found out I was pregnant again, for the fourth time in just ten short months, I knew that pregnancy would be different. The Lord had used me to comfort my friend, and in the process, He had healed so much of my brokenness. I was seeking Him faithfully daily. I was almost prideful, thinking I had nothing left to learn from loss. I was wrong. There was still so much to learn, and that came with losing our fourth angel baby.

My husband will tell you that the four angel babies we lost in ten months were souls God is preparing for a Revelation fight. While this may help my husband and his analytically wired personality, he doesn't live in the lies that the enemy sneaks into the minds of a grieving mother.

Each loss brought me to my knees, petitioning our Lord for His will to be done in my life. And every time I experienced loss, I gained more profound knowledge that God works everything for good. Although my prayers are complex and sometimes confusing, I've asked the Lord to use my suffering for good and His Glory. He has shown up in that.

One common theme throughout Scripture is God's promise that He is present. This world is so full of valleys and suffering. These are the moments where I believe God allows suffering to change our lives radically for Him. These moments are given to us to help us realize, even in our comfortable

Christianity, that we cannot do this world without Him. Valleys allow for the most intimate moments of petition with our Creator. In these moments, the world slows—and sometimes even stops—leaving us alone in the presence of our Lord.

Scripture describes the valley season in Psalm 23:4 *Even though I walk through the darkest valley, I will fear no evil, for you are with me; your rod and your staff, they comfort me.* (NIV) God is with us in the valley. He is comforting us in the valley. He is leading us in the valley. We have no reason to fear because He is with us.

James 1:12 tells us *Blessed is the one who perseveres under trial because, having stood the test, that person will receive the crown of life that the Lord has promised to those who love him.* (NIV) In order to persevere, we have to withstand trials. Without the testing of faith, how do we know if our faith exists? If we lived a life of ease without struggles, we would never have to reach up and seek God. Having been tested through this journey of loss and grief, God gave me the knowledge of an eternal perspective.

Children who are born into heaven never have to experience the suffering and the pain of this world. As a parent, our ultimate goal is to make disciples through our children. We want them to be born again into the kingdom of heaven. But what about those who are never born into the physical world but are born straight into heaven? If our goal is to have these children with us in our eternity with our Creator, didn't we succeed even though we never met them first?

When talking about fertility, Hannah is a biblical woman who likely comes to mind. When dealing with my personal grief of loss, I took a look back at Hannah. One thing I noticed about Hannah was her honesty. *Hannah replied, "I am a woman who is deeply troubled. I have not been drinking wine or beer; I was pouring out my soul to the LORD. Do not take your servant for a wicked woman; I have been praying here out of my great anguish and grief."* (1 Samuel 1:15-16 NIV) A few verses later, the Lord grants Hannah's prayer, and we find the commonly quoted verse, *"I prayed for this child."* (1 Samuel 1:27 NIV)

"I've been praying here out of my great anguish and grief." Hannah's words describe the feeling of pregnancy loss with the perfect adjectives: anguish and grief. We know Hannah's story has a happy ending as she bears a son she names Samuel. But what about the women who are still waiting on their happy ending? What about those who never receive the blessing of children and their desired "happy ending" doesn't happen this side of heaven? What if we aren't rewarded for persevering amidst suffering until we are in eternity with our Father?

Allow me to change the dialogue and ask a different question. What if our dark moments of suffering offer us the perfect opportunity to lead souls to the Father? Losing a child mid-pregnancy could offer a blessed chance to persevere through suffering and, ultimately, meet someone in *their* pain, giving them the gift of being seen and heard and understood. And what if your understanding heart points someone else to the understanding heart of Jesus Himself?

When my dad passed away at the early age of 61, I felt as if nobody could relate to me—until someone did. When someone who had been through a similar situation allowed me to feel seen and heard, my grief was validated and my healing began. Today I find great joy in helping others with the struggle of losing a parent. I love to listen and hear stories and even enjoy sharing a few of my own stories as we comfort and understand one another.

But with the stigma and dismissal associated with miscarriages, women are often left to suffer alone in silence. And it can be so hard to find the joy of the Lord in silence.

Hannah cried out in the depths of her anguish. She bore her soul to the Lord, and the Lord fulfilled her cries. She had promised the Lord to dedicate her child to Him, and she did. Her son Samuel went on to become a great man of God. Yet Hannah still experienced pain and suffering despite gaining what she had petitioned the thrones of heaven for. We serve a faithful God who fulfills His promises to us. If He said it would be, it will be. And although it is almost never the way we would like it to look, His plan is always greater than we can imagine.

Psalm 29:11 states, *The LORD gives His people strength; the LORD blesses His people with peace.* (NIV) Peace in your soul allows the presence of God's joy. If we allow ourselves to be honest with what we feel in moments of grief and pour out our emotions to our Father, He will be with us. It is promised in His Word.

The enemy seeks to bury us in guilt and shame, using both to isolate us and punish us. But there is to be no guilt or shame associated with miscarriage. By allowing ourselves to be vulnerable and openly share our testimony with others, they and we will be able to recognize that we are not alone. When we fellowship and support each other, God will use us to be a light in each other's darkness, clearly illuminating the fact that the devil himself is responsible for our feelings of condemnation or inadequacy. The enemy works hard to make us feel alone and stop the communion that comes when two women share their experiences and struggles. That is where iron sharpens iron and healing occurs.

When I set out to write my testimony of miscarriage, I knew this was the story the Lord wanted me to share, so I was obedient. I didn't realize, however, how God would bless me through sharing in *Joy Unspeakable*. I am overjoyed to tell you that the Lord blessed me with another pregnancy. I am currently 25 weeks along and having a healthy pregnancy. My husband

and I are looking forward to holding our baby boy, who is due on May 11, 2023. Even with all going well, I've had to fight through an emotional roller coaster as I have continued to learn more about fully trusting God.

Because another hidden fact about miscarriage is that pregnancy after loss is difficult. For the first two weeks, every time I used the restroom, I was terrified to look. Then, after I made it further than the previous four pregnancies and my nausea went full speed, I became dehydrated and visited the emergency room because of some of the symptoms I was experiencing. Pregnancy after loss is a spiritual battle. It's pushing through the feelings of worry. It's believing in God's promises and allowing His plan to unfold for His glory in my life. When we see a dead-end road, God sees the way out. The enemy likes to remind us of what was lost and tries to cloud our judgment with fear. Every passing week, I've rejoiced and experienced healing. The babies we lost will never be forgotten. I thank Jesus for each of them and the lessons I've learned in their absence.

Joy Unspeakable, regardless of your circumstances, is finding your true identity as a daughter of the King. It is looking through the trials and tribulations that come your way, trusting that God has the perfect plan. The joy of the Lord comes from living faithfully and seeking the answers to your questions while putting one foot in front of the other in obedience, even when you don't fully understand. Our joy is rooted in the firm foundation of knowing that this world is earthly and our King reigns forever seated high through the gates of heaven. As a daughter of that perfect King, you can feel joy even in pain, knowing God is using it all to catapult you and those around you into a blessed eternity with Him.

Joy in Overcoming

When we sit back and ponder the word "overcoming," we realize it carries a heavy weight. It means there is a battle to be fought—that something in your life must be overcome. But wrapped up in this word is a strength that comes from Jesus. A power that is supernatural because you fought the battle to overcome. When David fought Goliath, he knew he had to overcome a giant. (1 Samuel 17) I wish I could have been in David's head to hear the thoughts that must have entered his mind. He knew he had the strength of Jesus, but as a human, I am sure the question of how he could defeat this massive giant crossed his mind. But David chose to overcome. He stepped out in faith. He stepped out in trust.

Our lives are a lot like David's. When we face adversity, we often wonder how we will be an overcomer. The answer is that our focus must be on Jesus. There is joy when we overcome the most difficult circumstances, but those battles are not there just to be conquered; they are there to help us see what God can do when we depend on Him in our most challenging moments. 1 Samuel 17:48 states, *When the Philistine arose and came and drew near to meet David, David ran quickly toward the battle line to meet the Philistine.* (ESV) This visual brings great clarity that David was so ready and equipped with the power of God to overcome the giant in front of him. We can have joy in our battles by being ready—equipped with the power and Word of God. Battles are not always in our plan, but God can use giants that come against us to prepare and teach us how He has already overcome them through the blood of Jesus.

In your personal life, you may have faced many giants that you honestly had no idea how you would overcome, but God gently reminds us we are not on our own. Psalm 28:7 says, *The Lord is my strength and my shield; in him my heart trusts, and I am helped; my heart exults, and with my song, I give thanks to him.* (ESV) Just like David reached into his bag for a stone to attack the giant in front of him, no matter what giants we face, we can reach into our bag and grasp joy, strength, and God's armor. Running to the King of kings and Lord of lords as we are called to battle brings joy. Just like David ran quickly to face Goliath, we can run boldly to face what is in front of us. God works all things out for our good to build our confidence for the next battle. His joy in our hearts fights the enemy, and we can overcome all our battles with the strength of the Lord.

. . . .

Robert Thompson

Robert Thompson is a retired mentor/consultant for Men's Ministry. He holds a BA degree in Education from Hastings College, Hastings, Nebraska.

After ten years of teaching and coaching, Bob returned to help in his family's plumbing business. During this time, he obtained his Master Plumbing License.

In 1985 Bob moved to Durham, North Carolina, where he was called into ministry. His initial calling was ministering to men, where he has served for over 37 years. In 2000 he obtained his chaplaincy training through the Florida Baptist Convention Disaster Relief Program. This helped him pursue working in the local detention centers as a Bible study teacher. That position led him to become a chaplain and team leader for Truckstop Ministries working at the Flying J location in San Antonio, Florida.

In 2018 Bob learned he had stage IV colon cancer and has been fighting the disease ever since. Currently, he is a volunteer patient advocate in two of the FCS clinics helping other patients navigate through their cancer treatments spiritually.

What Cancer Can't Do

by Robert Thompson

Over the last several years, I have comforted many Christians who faced cancer and have always had the sense that should I be diagnosed, I would be prepared to handle it. You see, as a child working in my parents' heating business, I used to mix asbestos by hand. So, for the last 55+ years, I expected to receive a cancer diagnosis. And my strength held, even back in 1977, when my oldest son was diagnosed with cancer at the age of five.

But in April 2018, my life changed forever when I heard the doctor say to me, "We found a tumor. You have cancer." The next sentence was, "It is stage IV colorectal cancer, and it has metastasized in your liver." As I have clung to our sovereign God through my battle, I can now definitively declare that the joy of the Lord transcends even cancer.

God was with me when the word cancer became part of my routine, changing everything—when I began the fight of a lifetime as my world was blown apart. Despite what I was going through, I felt God's presence on this most horrible of days. He began to show me life was much deeper and held untold treasures that, without my diagnosis, I would never have seen. How ironic that cancer could show me a different way.

The surgeon felt uncomfortable performing immediate surgery because my cancer was so close to the rectal area. In retrospect, it might have been easier on me had he proceeded rather than waiting until May 2019 because of everything I had to endure during that time, but I trust that God had a plan.

As I processed my diagnosis, I didn't show much emotion, and my wife often asked me how I was doing. During this time, I prayed daily, never asking God, "Why me?" but instead asking, "Why not me?" Back in 1977, when my son was sick, I had made a covenant with God. I promised Him that if He cured my son, I would serve Him. Therefore, I assumed I needed to endure this cancer to be a better witness for Him and serve Him better.

I realized early on that I would face pain, infusions, horrific side effects, port surgery, CT scans every three months, and MRI and PET scans. I constantly prayed to God, asking Him to allow me to go through what I needed to so I could help others walk their road with cancer. I searched the scriptures for verses expressing what cancer can't do or take away so I could share those with others. I learned to approach life by taking each step with purpose. I began to recognize that every day is an opportunity to fight and never give up, to use what time we have to understand and simplify. We can each leave an indisputable mark on this earth; one way to establish that mark is to leave a legacy of kindness, love, and joy.

I learned firsthand that at any stage after a cancer diagnosis, one may experience times of distress and feel a range of strong emotions, such as disbelief, fear, anxiety, anger, and sadness. If we let them, these emotions can hold us back from the freedom offered in Christ. Jesus said it best in Luke 12:25-26, *"Can all your worries add a single moment to your life? And if worry can't accomplish a little thing like that, what's the use of worrying over bigger things?"* (NLT)

> *For God has not given us a spirit of fear, but of power and of love and of a sound mind.* (2 Timothy 1:7 NKJV)

As a believer, I had to remember that cancer could not take away the Spirit's abiding ministry to my heart and life. When cancer blindsides you, it is normal for the mind to spin with questions and uncertainties. But amid the turmoil, there is a place to turn, someone to go to for immediate help. *God is our refuge and strength, an ever-present help in trouble. Therefore we will not fear, though the earth give way and the mountains fall into the heart of the sea.* (Psalm 46:1-2 NIV)

Christians who have learned to suffer well often say something along these lines: "I would not have chosen my suffering, but now I would not give up what I learned in the process. God met me. My faith became real." Even a life-threatening diagnosis can be a blessing full of spiritual growth.

Additionally, cancer alone can not steal away the joy in your heart if you rely on God. The apostle Paul teaches us to rejoice. And he means it so much that he repeats himself. Rejoice in the Lord always. *Again I will say, Rejoice.* (Philippians 4:4 NKJV) As Christians, our joy is not dependent on outward circumstances. Real joy can never be stolen away by a disease. Real joy comes from having a relationship with our Lord and Savior, Jesus Christ. This doesn't mean that one who is enduring the trials of a disease rejoices *because* of his suffering, but it means God gives us the gift of being able to rejoice despite our suffering. The joy of the Lord is an inner attitude that, if we hold close to God, no one and nothing can take away.

> *Be glad in the LORD and rejoice, you righteous; and shout for joy, all you upright in heart!* (Psalm 32:11 NKJV)

As a person who has endured the disruption and even angst caused by cancer, I can say that it is normal—and okay—to become frustrated at the effects of cancer on the body. God gave us our bodies as a gift, and it can be psychologically painful to see God's gift ravaged. But what we must remember is that our soul is also a gift. And our soul will live on for eternity—unscathed by the world, protected by our God. While cancer can infiltrate our bodies, it can never touch our souls.

After my first year of chemotherapy, I mentioned to my oncologist that I wished his practice had patient advocates, especially for spiritual needs. His response was he had no problem with me speaking to anyone who was worried, anxious, fearful, confused, and hopeless. Having been blessed to have helped so many people in the past, I knew God had prepared me to handle not only my cancer but also the concerns of others.

God orchestrated my cancer so that I reached a point where I had the crutch knocked out from under my heart, causing me to trust in Him alone. This experience enabled me to start conversations with my health providers and fellow patients. I quickly learned that my doctors and nurses often suffered from "compassion fatigue." Through my illness, I knew I was being called to uphold the weary caregivers. They were thankful for my prayers and concern for their well-being. The infusion nurses always made a point to come by my chair to chat, both giving me solace and seeking their own as they, quite often, asked for prayers for family and loved ones. As our relationships developed, they would also drop hints as to whom I should talk with, giving me further opportunities to share my joy, which came naturally from my dependence on my relationship with God.

As I've fought this disease over the last four years, I have had the glorious opportunity to meet many patients and engage them in meaningful conversations. Many learned, by leaning into the Lord, to release their worry and anxiety. I encouraged them to overcome their fear by giving their concerns to God in prayer and resting in His provision. Through their release, they could open a space for the joy of the Lord to settle in their hearts.

> *"My peace I give to you; not as the world gives do I give to you. Let not your heart be troubled, neither let it be afraid."* (John 14:27 NKJV)

And as they drew closer to the Lord, many became thankful for their trials, recognizing that through those trials, God allowed them to become more dependent on Him. When we experience the weakness of the soul or flesh and lean on God, He shows us that His grace is enough. And in Him, our weakness is made strong.

> *And He said to me, "My grace is sufficient for you, for My strength is made perfect in weakness." Therefore most gladly I will rather boast in my infirmities, that the power of Christ may rest upon me.* (2 Corinthians 12:9 NKJV)

Here are a few more thoughts that I have often left with my fellow patients:

- At my lowest, God is my hope.
  May the God of hope fill you with all joy and peace in believing, that you may abound in hope by the power of the Holy Spirit. (Romans 15:13 NKJV)

- At my darkest, God is my light.
  When I sit in darkness, the Lord will be a light to me. (Micah 7:8 NKJV)

- At my weakest, God is my strength.
  But those who wait on the Lord
  Shall renew their strength;
  They shall mount up with wings like eagles,
  They shall run and not be weary,
  They shall walk and not faint.
  (Isaiah 40:31 NKJV)

- At my saddest, God is my comforter.
  "Let not your heart be troubled." (John 14:1 NKJV)

And of His fullness we have all received, and grace for grace. (John 1:16 NKJV)

God's grace continually meets and upholds us. No disease can stop God's power. The Bible promises us that not only can we approach God with our needs, but that He will always respond. *Let us therefore come boldly to the throne of grace, that we may obtain mercy and find grace to help in time of need.* (Hebrews 4:16 NKJV)

Holding tight to our Christianity—that is, holding tight to our relationship with God—carries us through any circumstance that may come our way.

Through my own experience with cancer and through the gift of walking with others, I have learned that even the devastating effects of cancer cannot stop God's purpose in our lives. God is always working. Nothing happens by chance, but everything is ordained by God. The Bible reminds us of this often.

> *In Him also we have obtained an inheritance, being predestined according to the purpose of Him who works all things according to the counsel of His will, that we who first trusted in Christ should be to the praise of His glory.* (Ephesians 1:11-12 NKJV)

Our God is sovereign, which means He is in control of everything in our lives—even cancer.

Despite anything that comes against us unexpectedly, we can trust that God is in charge and nothing surprises Him. Therefore, regardless of how we feel, we can rest in His presence and accept His peace. God will use even our most difficult situations for our spiritual benefit and good. When we yield to Him, He will also use our circumstances to position and prepare us to serve Him and others. By leaning into God's sovereignty and trusting His purpose, we can be infiltrated with peace and joy beyond our human understanding.

The Holy Spirit shared with me early on my journey that God was going to teach me a lot about how to trust Him more and minister to other cancer patients and doctors. One thing I learned during my chaplaincy training was never to tell anyone that you understand what they are going through unless you have walked that same journey. And never assume or state that you know how someone is feeling, as each person's circumstance is unique.

I started my journey at one of the larger clinics, where there were a total of approximately 50 infusion chairs. This gave me a large area to cover each time I received treatment. During one of my early conversations with my doctor, I learned that they did not have a patient advocate for spiritual well-being. The doctor said I was free to help comfort patients as the opportunity arose.

When my wife heard this, she commented that I had never met a stranger. I kept my reading material, including my Bible, on the side arm where all the patients and infusion nurses could see. Many noticed and asked questions as they walked by.

With my 37+ years of experience ministering to others, I knew it would take weeks and even months for the men to build enough confidence in our relationship to ask questions. Women, on the other hand, being emotional by nature, asked me questions almost within the first few minutes of our conversations. We talked about many of the things I mentioned earlier, such as worry, anxiety, fear, hopelessness, and faith. The other patients would almost always ask why a loving God would allow a horrible disease such as cancer to affect their lives. The nurses would also ask questions, often about God and how He was working in their own lives. I couldn't help but recognize the spiritual thirst prevalent in so many lives.

Recently I have been able to receive some of my infusions and lab work at a closer and smaller clinic, so now God has provided me with a new group of people to share His light with. Once I was leaving the clinic with my "fanny pack" chemo pump on my waist when I noticed a caregiver,"Jess," who looked worn out. I asked if I could pray for her and speak more with her on my next trip. As God would have it, my pump failed when I got home, so back to the clinic I went to exchange pumps. Guess who helped me? Jess. God has such a sense of humor and is so in control. We were able to speak as Jess, who I now saw was the pharmacist/lab technician, changed out my pump.

I am so thankful to God for these experiences of meeting patients and medical personnel. This cancer, which began ravaging my body back in 2018, has given me far more than it has taken away from me.

Cancer has given me a greater dependence on God's provision as He and I fight this disease together.

Cancer has allowed me to relate to and uphold many other Christian patients going through previously unimaginable circumstances.

Cancer has given me the opportunity to step into the lives of many caregivers, offering them my prayers and biblical encouragement.

Cancer has provided me with a unique mission field where I've been able to plant many seeds, teaching of God's glory.

And cancer has gifted me with the realization that true joy never comes from our circumstances, but comes as a byproduct of our relationship with Jesus Christ.

I don't know what you are going through in this season that threatens to steal your joy, and I won't pretend to understand what you are going through. But I know that our God is the true and only provider of joy and peace and that by holding to Him, you, too, can have joy unspeakable—regardless of *your* circumstance. God bless you!

Joy in Eternal Security

Have you ever doubted your salvation? Or your eternal security? Have you questioned your own sincerity in asking Jesus Christ into your heart to be your Lord and Savior? Maybe you've wondered how you could be certain you are saved. The very fact that you are asking these questions is a good sign that Christ has claimed you as His own.

From the moment we ask Jesus into our heart, the enemy constantly tries to convince us that we are not saved and are not worthy to be saved. He plants doubts and fears into our mind to confuse us and keep us from being effective for Jesus. The very fact that you have doubts confirms that the enemy is relentlessly attacking you because you are no longer his—you belong to Jesus! Your fears and doubts are not from God (2 Timothy 1:7) but are from the pit of hell! God is life-giving, but the enemy tries to steal your joy. Jesus tells us, *"The thief comes only to steal and kill and destroy; I have come that they may have life, and have it to the full."* (John 10:10 NIV)

But how can I be worthy enough to enter God's kingdom? Entering God's kingdom has never been dependent on who we are—we can only enter through God's grace! In John 3:15-16, God explains that the way to Him is through the gift of His Son, Jesus. And He promises that all who believe in Jesus Christ will be granted eternal life. And God cannot lie or back out of His promises. (Numbers 23:19) So we can stand on the truth and in agreement with the enemy when he accuses us of not being worthy, thanking him for reminding us that *only* God is worthy—"WORTHY IS THE LAMB!" (Revelation 5:12 NIV)

But what about when we sin? Can sin destroy our chance at salvation? Ephesians 2:8-9 reveals that our salvation is a gift from God that we cannot earn. If we don't have the power to gain salvation for ourselves, we certainly can't do anything to lose it. In John 10:28-29, Jesus Christ declared, *"I give them eternal life, and they shall never perish; no one will snatch them out of my hand. My Father, who has given them to me, is greater than all; no one can snatch them out of my Father's hand."* (NIV)

God keeps His children eternally secure through His power. When we accept Jesus Christ as our Savior, God guarantees our eternal security. Jude celebrated this—and so can we! *To him who is able to keep you from stumbling and to present you before his glorious presence without fault and with great joy.* (Jude 1:24 NIV)

Wow! There is no one more powerful than Jesus and the Father, who is the same. The enemy is optimistic, thinking he can snatch you out of God's hand. But no matter how hard he tries to steal your joy by planting seeds of doubt and fear, he doesn't have the power to take away your eternal security.

Once saved, nothing can separate us from the love of God or take away our eternal security. Paul explains this in Romans 8:38-39, *For I am convinced that neither death nor life, neither angels nor demons, neither the present nor the future, nor any powers, neither height nor depth, nor anything else in all creation, will be able to separate us from the love of God that is in Christ Jesus our Lord.* (NIV).

And the apostle John confirms that those who know Jesus can be confident of spending eternity with God. *God has given us eternal life, and this life is in His Son. ...I write these things to you who believe in the name of the Son of God so that you may know that you have eternal life.* (1 John 5:11,13 NIV)

Shout hallelujah! As a Christ-follower, you can stand joyfully with complete confidence in God's promise for an eternity secure in His presence.

· ·

Terry Perches

As an award-winning real estate professional, author, speaker, and community leader, Terry Perches has been impacting the lives of others for many years. Her resilience, compassion, and faith make her one of the top female business professionals in the marketplace today. Terry's personal story of trials and triumph continues to inspire all who hear it.

Terry is a Residential Real Estate Professional specializing in marketing, consulting, and education. She interviews and qualifies buyer and seller prospects. Additionally, she is a certified Seller Representative Specialist and Military Relocation Professional.

Terry loves and believes in serving and giving back to her community. She has had the privilege, honor, and opportunity to be involved in several organizations. These include her church and women's ministry, Fort Hunter Firehouse Women's Auxiliary (serving as an Emergency Feeding Officer), Circle of Champs (helping children with life-threatening illnesses), and Juvenile and Women's Facilities (as a mentor, chaplain, and Bible study lead). She has held officer roles with Guilderland High School Booster Club and Pasco Federated Republican Women's Club. Additionally, Terry has served on the boards of Stonecroft Christian Women's Club and The Umbrella of the Capital District and was named Ambassador of the Year by Central Pasco Chamber of Commerce.

Involvement in all these ministries and organizations has been very rewarding and has given Terry an extensive education in serving, teaching, and meeting the needs of those in her sphere of influence. Her experiences have also taught her many valuable lessons on building trust, confidence, and loyalty to those she has had the privilege to serve.

Broken Pieces Made Whole

by Terry Perches

Broken Pieces

Life shattered, broken dreams, life in shambles—can you relate? How did I get to this point in my life? How did I end up here with absolutely nothing to live for? Is this all there is to life? What is my purpose?

These questions ran through my mind as I sat there watching my drug dealer sell drugs to everyone who showed up at his doorstep. I was physically sick that day from the weekend drug party and felt like my life was over. *This is how I'm going to die,* I thought to myself. I was only 27 years old, with no hope or thoughts of any future. Lost and alone, walking in the path of destruction, with no one who truly loved or cared for me. I had lost everything, including my two beautiful children.

I am sharing my story with the desire that it might help someone and bring hope to this lost and dying world. I want to help others see there is a way out of the destructive path they are on. No matter where you currently are, you can live a life of freedom and joy and have a fulfilling life and purpose.

I was born in East Los Angeles, California. My mom was only 16 when she gave birth to me. I was an unwanted pregnancy. I later learned after she passed away that she had tried to abort the life inside her. I believe that had abortion been legal, I would not be here today to share my story. But God had other plans. *For you created my inmost being; you knit me together in my mother's womb. I praise you because I am fearfully and wonderfully made; your works are wonderful.* (Psalm 139:13-14 NIV)

I lived with my maternal grandmother. I loved my mom and always wanted to live with her, but every time I went home with her, it ended poorly. By age 12, I had been abused by two of her husbands. So back to grandma's place I would go. My mom died at 40 years old from cirrhosis of the liver due to her alcoholism.

My grandmother raised me to the best of her ability. Being a single woman herself and a business owner, she had a lot to deal with. She was not your typical grandma! My grandmother owned a little neighborhood bar in East Los Angeles on Brooklyn Ave. Obviously, I didn't have many friends coming over to play. I saw things no child should have been exposed to and was told not to discuss them.

She once told me that she only had a 4th-grade education. And the only reason she made it to the 4th grade was that she was too big for the desk, so they had to pass her from the lower grades. Grandma was funny and a woman ahead of her time, very smart and witty, a businesswoman! We lived in the back of the bar in a small room with only a twin bed, sink, stove, refrigerator, small closet, and an ironing board. She owned the bar until I was 13 years old.

I remember trips we would take after she closed the bar. Grandma would wake me up around two in the morning to go visit friends and family in Lompoc, Mexico, and other places. We would drive for hours in her gray Pontiac, with windows down, listening to loud music all the way to help her stay awake. I loved music, maybe because we had a jukebox in the bar with so many songs to choose from. When I was small, I remember dancing and singing on the bar counter for all her customers. I aspired to be the next Shirley Temple. My grandmother enrolled me in dance lessons and I loved it! Some of my most memorable and fun times were events where I danced and sang on stage for executives.

Growing up, I had some good times and many bad experiences. I ran away from home three times.

The first time I ran away from my grandmother was after she sold the bar. Within one year, we moved several times, eventually ending up in a motel room. I hated living there; my grandmother would often go out drinking and leave me alone. So I left to stay with one of my friend's family. I don't know how my grandmother found me, but she did and brought me back to the motel. That night after going out, she came back drunk and pulled a knife on me. I talked her into putting it down, but she was so angry at me for running away that she picked up one of my sandals and hit me on the head over and over again. I still have a scar on my head from that incident. The next morning, a male friend of hers stopped by the motel. I answered the door with my head and face still covered in dried blood from the sandal beating. My grandmother also came to the door, immediately sending me to take a shower. When I came out, her friend was gone.

The second time I ran away, I left with a few so-called friends from school. All we did was run the streets and get high. When I got caught, my mom and grandmother decided to put me in a juvenile detention center, believing this would scare me and straighten me out. It didn't work; it only made me more rebellious! By the time I was 15 years old, I went from drinking and smoking cigarettes to smoking pot, taking pills, and hallucinogenic drugs.

On my third run from home, I was staying at my mom's apartment. One day, my grandmother happened to stop by and was not pleased to find me home high on drugs. She started yelling and threatened to tell my mom. I made my way out of the apartment through the bathroom window and left again. This time, one month before my 16th birthday, I hooked up with some older friends, and we made it to Woodstock! Those memories are vague, but I do remember mud, some rain, Jimi Hendrix, and Janis Joplin. When I returned home that time around, my mom called the police to our apartment, had me arrested, and I was sent back to juvenile hall. When I was released, I came back to my mom's place. I tried to behave and get back to school. However, I began hanging out with the wrong crowd again and quit school after the 9th grade.

I married at the age of 16. I do NOT recommend this to anyone! My mom and grandmother had enough of my rebellion and didn't know what else to do with me. They encouraged me to get married, hoping this would straighten me out. So I married a guy from the old neighborhood. He was four years older than me, so I figured, why not? We had gone out several times, and I thought he loved me. I did not know what real love was, nor did I have a good model of a healthy family. I knew I wanted a family like the Cleavers on the TV show *Leave It to Beaver*, where the wife stayed home, cooked, cleaned, and cared for the children while the husband worked and lovingly took care of his family. That didn't work out as I envisioned! I had two beautiful daughters by the time I was 19 years old, but I was only married for four years. During that time, I stayed clean, with no drugs or alcohol use, so I guess he did help me in that area. But I caught him smoking pot in the garage several times and left him for being unfaithful.

So at the age of 20, I moved back to my mom's, hoping to find a job and get on my feet. Finally, I found a job and started working for a paper company. I was young, just turned 21, and ready to party after four years of playing house. So I started going out to bars with co-workers. One night I didn't come home until the morning, and when I did, I found my mom passed out from pills and my two and four-year-old daughters sitting there with the pills on the coffee table and no supervision! That was a wake-up call for me. I knew my mom tried to help me, but with her drug and alcohol addiction, she was just not capable. I realized I could no longer stay there and expose my girls to the lifestyle I was brought up in. So I moved in with my stepdad, but his current wife, whom my mom introduced him to, was not happy about this living arrangement. I didn't help the situation by coming in late after having a few drinks with co-workers. Needless to say, we didn't live there long. With no one and nowhere to go, I ended up living in the same motel where I lived with my grandmother; you know, the motel I hated! It was a very difficult time trying to work, find a babysitter, and live in one room with no kitchen and two kids. I decided to ask their dad to help me during the week since he was unemployed and living at his parent's house. That was a BIG mistake, beginning a 6-year battle to see my girls.

Neither my ex-husband nor his parents would allow me to see my daughters during that time. His family would slam the door in my face and say I wasn't my children's mother. One year during those six years, my ex moved out of his parents' home and in with his girlfriend. During that time, I had an opportunity to see my girls, but then they were taken away and not allowed to see me for other reasons. These were heartbreaking times for me. I continued to party, burying all the hurt deep within my hardened heart with more drinking and stronger drugs. I was so lost and blind, walking on the path of destruction!

But destruction will come to the workers of iniquity. (Proverbs 10:29 NKJV)

My cousin and I were very close and hung out a lot together, but we were not good influences on each other. She had a friend, Ronnie, who really liked her. His life had changed, and he would share what God had done in his life. He even bought my cousin a Bible. She kept the Bible in her room, and one day, before heading out to score drugs and get high, I picked it up and read a passage: *For the lips of an immoral woman drip honey, And her mouth is smoother than oil; But in the end she is bitter as wormwood, Sharp as a two-edged sword.* (Proverbs 5:3-4 NKJV)

I had no clue what that meant! My cousin walked into the room as I was reading, and we both had a good laugh. I left to get high, but God was working on me! Another time, we got a ride from Ronnie, and he had Christian music playing. I didn't know it was Christian, but I liked the beat and especially the words that said, "I am the Freeway." I didn't understand what that meant, but it sounded so good and positive. I believe God was using this song to draw me to Himself.

Ronnie would come around once in a while and would invite us to church. I finally accepted his invitation, and when the day arrived, I called him up and tried to back out because I needed to get high. I was now using heroin and had the monkey on my back (hooked on drugs). I remember he said to me, "Don't let Satan rip you off."

I replied, "Then you better come get me now!" I was in a spiritual battle and didn't realize it. It was a battle for my soul.

I was a liar, thief, murderer (I had two abortions), addicted to drugs, in bondage, blind to the truth, lost, and hopeless. But God!!! His grace and mercy brought me to a saving knowledge of Himself and set me upon a rock.

> *The Lord is my rock and my fortress and my deliverer; My God, my strength, in whom I will trust; My shield and the horn of my salvation, my stronghold.* (Psalm 18:2 NKJV)

With no future to look forward to and no hope, God gave me hope and a future. *For I know the thoughts that I think toward you, says the LORD, thoughts of peace and not of evil, to give you a future and a hope. Then you will call upon Me and go and pray to Me, and I will listen to you. And you will seek Me and find Me, when you search for Me with all your heart.* (Jeremiah 29:11-13 NKJV)

Made Whole!

When I went to church that night, I had an encounter with Jesus. He became my Savior and changed my life forever! When I repented, prayed for forgiveness, and accepted Him into my heart, He forgave me for all my sins. I was now a child of God, amen!

> *I called on the LORD in distress; The LORD answered me and set me in a broad place.* (Psalm 118:5 NKJV)

> *He also brought me up out of a horrible pit, Out of the miry clay, And set my feet upon a rock, And established my steps.* (Psalm 40:2 NKJV)

That day in September 1980 was the last time I ever got high, smoked, drank, or fornicated. Not only was I now saved, forgiven, and assured of heaven, but I was also totally healed and never went through withdrawals, which I know does not happen for everyone. I did not go to any rehab, Alcoholics Anonymous, or a 12-step program. He made me whole in Him immediately, and I did not look back.

I took one step of faith in Jesus and believed in the God of the universe who created me and knew me intimately!

> *For You formed my inward parts; You covered me in my mother's womb. I will praise You, for I am fearfully and wonderfully made; Marvelous are Your works, And that my soul knows very well. My frame was not hidden from You, When I was made in secret, And skillfully wrought in the lowest parts of the earth. Your eyes saw my substance, being yet unformed. And in Your book they all were written, The days fashioned for me, When as yet there were none of them.* (Psalm 139:13-16 NKJV)

This is what God has done for me: He saved me from my sin, washed and cleansed me, and made me whole in Him. I was no longer in bondage to sin; I was able to say NO because I was now filled with His Holy Spirit!!

I want my life's story to show how God took a broken, unwanted, drug-addicted woman and gave her hope and joy and another chance in life. I desire to lead people to the Lord by sharing the truth of the gospel. I want God to use my story to help others suffering from addictions.

> *Then I will teach transgressors Your ways, and sinners shall be converted to You. Deliver me from the guilt of bloodshed, O God, The God of my salvation, and my tongue shall sing aloud of Your righteousness. O Lord, open my lips, And my mouth shall show forth Your praise.* (Psalm 51:13-15 NKJV)

> *He has put a new song in my mouth—Praise to our God; Many will see it and fear, And will trust in the LORD.* (Psalm 40:3 NKJV)

Over my lifetime, I have seen God's faithfulness toward me in many ways! I would never have imagined the path He chose for me or how He has gently and graciously led me. God has brought so many unexpected changes, surprises, provisions, and opportunities at just the right time!

> *You will show me the path of life; In Your presence is fullness of joy; At Your right hand are pleasures forevermore.* (Psalm 16:11 NKJV)

God has been and is so good to me! With God's help and a Christian attorney, I was able to reconnect with my two beautiful daughters and be part of their lives again. He also brought me a wonderful, faithful, godly husband who loves and cares for me. We have two children together and now have a total of 12 grandchildren!

God is a God of second and third chances. He restored all that the enemy tried to destroy. I am victorious in Him and more than a conqueror. God has turned the unspeakable things I did in my past to JOY Unspeakable in living a life pleasing to Him and sharing His love with those He brings into my life.

> *But thanks be to God, who gives us the victory through our Lord Jesus Christ.* (1 Corinthians 15:57 NKJV)

> *I will greatly rejoice in the LORD, my soul shall be joyful in my God; For He has clothed me with the garments of salvation.* (Isaiah 61:10a NKJV)

My prayer and hope for anyone reading this is that you will find Jesus, the author and finisher of our faith, who can set you free and give you eternal life.

If you have ever asked the same questions I asked myself, I'm here to tell you Jesus is the answer. He is the way, the truth, and the life!

I tried everything to drown out the pain, including suicide. But, by the grace of God, He heard my cry and rescued me. He will do the same for you. Surrender your life to Him and decide to accept Him today as your personal Lord and Savior.

If we confess our sins, He is faithful and just to forgive us our sins and to cleanse us from all unrighteousness. (1 John 1:9 NKJV)

For God so loved the world that He gave His only begotten Son, that whoever believes in Him should not perish but have everlasting life. (John 3:16 NKJV)

Nor is there salvation in any other, for there is no other name under heaven given among men by which we must be saved. (Acts 4:12 NKJV)

Joy in His Mercy & Grace

Many people believe they must clean up their lives before coming to God. They do not think they could ever be forgiven for the way they have lived. I once had a pastor whose favorite saying was, "You can't clean fish until you catch them." We are all sinners and incapable of cleaning up our lives on our own. Romans 3:23 says, *For all have sinned and fall short of the glory of God.* (NIV)

No matter how much we have sinned, we can have hope and the greatest joy of all! Because our God is loving, merciful, and gracious. *For God so loved the world that He gave His one and only Son, that whoever believes in Him shall not perish but have eternal life. For God did not send His Son into the world to condemn the world, but to save the world through Him.* (John 3:16-17 NIV)

Do you see how much God loves us? He doesn't want to condemn us. He loves us so much that He sent His Son, Jesus Christ, to live and then die on the cross for our sins so that we can have a relationship with Him and clean up our lives with His help.

Whether our sin is big or small, it is still a sin. And we must pay the penalty for our sins. The Bible says *For the wages of sin is death, but the gift of God is eternal life in Christ Jesus our Lord.* (Romans 6:23 NIV) God is a just God, but He is merciful and gives us grace if we believe and trust in Jesus Christ and what Jesus did for us on the cross. (Romans 10:9)

Mercy means not getting the punishment we deserve: separation from God forever (in hell).

Grace is unmerited favor, getting what we do not deserve: forgiveness for our sins—past, present, and future—allowing us to spend eternity with God in heaven.

> *God saved us because of His mercy and grace.* (Titus 3:5-7 NIV)

There are multiple examples of God's mercy and grace toward some of the great heroes of the Bible. King David is one example. He was known as a man after God's own heart, yet he lusted after and impregnated another man's wife and then had that man murdered so he could take his wife. Abraham, who lied, also received God's mercy. Abraham's wife, Sarah, was impatient and didn't trust God's promise; Jacob was known as a swindler; Moses disobeyed God; Rahab was a prostitute; Saul was a persecutor of Christians; and Peter denied Jesus three times. The list goes on, but you get the point. Despite their atrocious sins against Him, God gave His love, mercy, and grace to each of these individuals. And He offers His love, grace, and mercy to all of us, too. *For the grace of God has appeared that offers salvation to all people.* (Titus 6:11 NIV)

God's mercy and grace are free gifts through faith, as stated in Ephesians 2:8-9 *For it is by grace you have been saved, through faith—and this is not from yourselves, it is the gift of God—not by works, so that no one can boast.* (NIV)

How can we not be joyful at the offer of such amazing gifts?

Stephanie Winslow

Stephanie Winslow is the proud wife of Marshall and mother of two girls, Cora and Lydia. Stephanie helps business and ministry professionals develop leadership and communication skills to help them grow into a life of significance, impact, and abundance. She founded her company, Blind Spot Consultants, in 2016. Recently, she became a John Maxwell team-certified coach, trainer, and speaker.

Stephanie's first book, *Ascent to Hope*, was published in 2018. She uses her gifts of writing, coaching, and speaking to inspire transformational change in the lives of those who need hope, healing, and restoration.

In her free time, Stephanie enjoys long walks on the beach, playing any sport or board game with her family, coffee dates with girlfriends, the comfort of a soft hoodie, and the pampering of pedicures.

Oil of Joy
By Stephanie Winslow

I took a long deep breath in, followed by a slow, intentional exhale.

"I feel like I have a physical hole in my chest! I can't seem to catch my breath," I explained. "I just keep holding my breath, hoping the aching of my heart will fade."

"Why does this have to be so hard? Why does this have to hurt so badly?"

My husband, Marshall, sat next to me as I lay curled up on our bed after another restless night. He held my hand as I cried, questioned, and talked.

The hole I felt in my chest was the weight of grief after my only brother, Zach, passed away. After Zach passed, I had several weeks of sleepless nights as I dreamt about all that was said and done. I rehearsed the events over and over. *What could we have done differently? Did I say everything I needed to say? Did he know for sure that I loved him?*

My heart and mind were spent. With my thoughts caught in a spine of replays, my emotions were stretched to a breaking point. As I sat with Marshall unpacking all that filled my head, trying to allow space for grieving, I realized just how uncomfortable the unfamiliar emptiness that loomed around us felt.

"Nothing is the same, Marshall. Nothing! My thoughts are different; my body is different; I move differently. I feel differently. I hear differently. I see things differently. Everything has changed. Nothing is the same. I am not the same."

The tears I thought were at bay began to slide down my raw cheeks.

"Even my tears are different," I whimpered.

And they were. They were heavier. They were more substantial. They were not just any tears.

"It's almost like these tears are made of oil," I said to Marshall. He wrapped me up in his arms and held me.

Later that night, apprehensive about my ability to fall asleep and desperate for good, sound sleep, I had Marshall pray over me.

Not unlike the nights before, I dreamed. But this time, I dreamed about the conversation I'd had with Marshall that morning about my oily tears.

In the dream, I saw myself kneeling, arms outstretched, face up to the sky, tears streaming down my face, and oil being poured out on my head from above.

This dream put meaning to my tears. This dream confirmed to me that, indeed, my tears were not just any tears. This dream gave purpose to the seemingly, unstoppable tears that made their resting place on my cheeks. My tears were combined with Jesus' anointing oil. They were tears of anointing oil.

As I cried out in sorrow, Jesus was meeting me, comforting me, holding my hand, and leading me through grief. He was treating the wounds of my heart and soul with His tender oil.

The following morning, I woke up and went about my regular routine. The devotion I read was the story in the Gospel of Luke, where the scandalous Mary knelt before Jesus. In this story we find Mary, a desperate and empty woman, seeking healing for her heart at the feet of Jesus. Luke describes how Mary washed Jesus' feet with her tears; then the broken woman dried them with her hair, kissed them, and covered them with expensive oil.

> *A woman in that town who lived a sinful life learned that Jesus was eating at the Pharisee's house, so she came there with an alabaster jar of perfume. As she stood behind Him at His feet weeping, she began to wet His feet with her tears. Then she wiped them with her hair, kissed them, and poured perfume on them.* (Luke 7:37-38 NIV)

Have you ever wondered how many tears it would have taken to wash Jesus' dusty feet? I had never thought much about it until I sat reading this story in light of my own continuous tears.

As I read the story of Mary's heart poured out before Jesus, it struck my own heart that she did not cry, but tears flowed from her—like a brimming cup that doesn't run dry. There was no end to the number of tears she could have cried. And oh, how I could relate to Mary.

I believe that as she approached Jesus, Mary's eyes were opened to the beauty and awesomeness of Jesus' love available to her. She was overwhelmed by His grace and love. She was overwhelmed to the point of releasing uninterrupted, grateful tears that would anoint her Savior's feet.

Mary's encounter with Jesus resonated with my own experience: the outpouring of oil and the outflow of tears.

God allowed me to experience the weightiness of my tears that led to the dream and then to the biblical story of old, all to show me that He saw me. He saw my tears, and He was drawing my heart to Him so that He could exchange my sorrow for joy.

I am awed by the love, grace, and goodness of Jesus. At times I am awed to tears, flowing tears. Jesus anointed my head with the oil of comfort, strength, peace, hope, and even joy. He allowed my tears to feel heavy, like oil as a balm to my soul. He showed me that He is here with me—in the discomfort of all that is different.

This dream and experience of flowing tears of oil happened almost three years ago. Yet I'm still getting used to the discomfort of missing my sibling. But the heaviness of my tears is the reassurance that God is pouring out His comfort and compassion on me. God understands the loss I feel more than anyone, as He gave up His only Son for my ransom.

God is with me in the heartache, continuing to pour out His oil even as I now grieve the passing of my mom, Bekki. I am again trusting Him with the hole in my heart, remembering the healing He provided before. I know God can and will heal me again.

Therefore, I continue to kneel before Him, seeking solace and peace from the only One who is able to make me whole. As the tears mix with the oil and flow down my cheeks, my soul is once again soothed with His healing presence. What a sight. What a feeling. What a picture this has become for me of His gentle grace.

His peace and grace are the beginning. In Isaiah, God speaks to us and declares what Jesus will do for us:

[Jesus will] *provide for those who grieve in Zion—to bestow on them a crown of beauty instead of ashes, the oil of joy instead of mourning, and a garment of praise instead of a spirit of despair. They will be called oaks of righteousness, a planting of the Lord for the display of His splendor.* (Isaiah 61:3 NIV)

Amid this verse rests the same word, "oil." He promises to exchange mourning for the "oil of joy."

We often hear in Christian circles that God doesn't waste anything. He doesn't waste our tears. He doesn't waste our mourning. After the last three years of bereavement, I know if we allow Him, God will use mourning to engage us in an exchange that will take us from sorrow to joy.

In the Bible, anointing oil was used to mark someone or something as "set apart." Priests were anointed with oil when assigned their role in the temple, signifying their separation from the world and God's hand on their lives.

In the same way, my tears of oil are symbolic of a life set apart for a purpose. God has used sorrow to "set apart" my heart and allow me the opportunity to experience joy and comfort in a way that I could not know or understand without this path.

Have you considered this? What if our tears, our hardships, and our struggles in this life are the very things that set us apart? What if they are the very things He uses to make us holy? What if all the challenges are the sharpening of our souls and spirits to lift us up to the calling He wants us to step into? What if the mourning of this life is to help us experience fuller joy?

As I contemplate these questions, my mom's tender eyes and sweet, radiant face come to mind. Mom was diagnosed with ovarian cancer in 2020, right at the beginning of the pandemic—only six months after my brother passed.

Toward the end of her life, ovarian cancer had eaten away at her body. These were difficult days as we faced another huge earthly loss for our family. Mom battled with chemo and cancer for nearly two years before her earthly body failed, and heaven welcomed a saint home.

Of all the people who touched my life, my mom is the one who consistently poured out the most peace and joy—even on the hardest days.

Laying bedridden for eight weeks, her life consisted of tubes, pumps, alarms sounding, doctors, surgeries, no solid food, medications, and isolation. Yet, despite this and everything going wrong in her physical body, God blessed her with resilient joy and gratitude.

When I visited her in the hospital, the nurses would say, "We have never had a patient like her. She is so upbeat and positive. She brings us joy when we should be lifting her up." Every nurse on the floor knew her; they were drawn to her.

Her doctors would ask us, "Does Bekki ever complain? It's hard to know when she isn't feeling well, isn't it?"

And our answer was, "No, she doesn't complain."

Mom would just say, "No sense in complaining; doesn't change a thing."

What does change things? If complaining doesn't?

Mom found the secret. She concentrated on God's faithfulness throughout her life. She focused her thoughts on all the blessings He had imparted to her. She shifted her eyes from her situation to all that was good, right, and true. She wasn't preoccupied with her pain but rather with the healing power of God.

And therefore, she could live these wearisome days, at peace and with joy, through the biggest challenges of her life.

In the last few weeks of my mom's life, I was blessed to sit next to her and hold her hand. During our treasured time together, she rarely spoke. She'd respond with a word or two when I asked a question. But for the most part, there was quiet as the sounds of soft piano music or the ruffling of HGTV played in the background.

In the sweetness of the silence, I often wondered what was going through her mind, contemplating what I might be thinking if I was in her place. I was quite certain I would not be handling things with the resolve, strength, and gratitude she displayed. I didn't know what to say as the nearness of the end of her race drew closer.

I rubbed her feet with sea salt and scented lotion—getting pedicures together had been a favorite activity of ours. She loved it. And I loved it. I loved being able to serve a woman who had taken brilliant care of me. I soaked up every moment I had with her.

Every day we were together, we held hands, and I rubbed her feet. She'd smile with tenderness, her eyes twinkling with hope and peace. It was as if all we needed to say had already been said in the months and years prior.

It was true. There was not a question in my mind about how she loved me. And I knew she did not question my love for her. I was blessed to have a mom who demonstrated love well and immeasurably in her words and actions.

One afternoon as I rubbed her feet, I thought she had dozed off. After a few minutes passed, I looked up at her to see if she was resting well, and there she was, looking at me with a gentle smile.

"What are you thinking, Mama?" I asked her.

Her smile broadened, and she looked me in the eyes and said, "I'm just grateful."

I smiled a tender smile back at her. I fought back the tears that began to well up. I turned my face and pressed my cheek to my shoulder. I tried to see through the tears and turned my focus back to rubbing her feet.

My tears won the fight and streamed down my cheeks, and as they dropped, they wetted her feet.

"Wow," I thought to myself, "she's grateful. Of all people. Gosh, I want to be just like her."

At that moment, I was wrapped up in God's loving arms, in His presence. He touched my heart.

My mom's faith, perspective, and gratitude awed me. And in turn, I was in awe of God for giving Rebecca Miller to me as my mom.

How blessed I felt. The tears streamed and continued to drop on her feet as I rubbed them.

When I climbed into bed that night, the dream I had after Zach passed away came to mind. Jesus poured His oil on my head, mixing it with my tears that wet my mom's feet. This moment with my mom was just that—a moment—but it was awe-inspiring as it reminded me of Mary at the feet of Jesus. It all came full circle.

I got to see Jesus, to feel His presence in a whole new light that day—at the bedside of my dying mom. Her pleasant demeanor and kindness in the most painful, unbelievable circumstance gave me a glimpse of what it must have been like to sit at Jesus' feet. This is what Mary must have felt as she knelt before Christ. I got to see Christ in the eyes of my mom.

Being with my mom in the quiet of God's presence, a new joy was birthed in me. It was a joy that was delivered from the simplest words. "I'm just grateful." It was not a joy that bubbled over in laughter. Instead, it was a joy that planted my roots of faith deeper into the foundation of Christ.

In Psalm 45:7, the psalmist declares, *You love righteousness and hate wickedness; therefore God, your God, has set you above your companions by anointing you with the oil of joy.* (NIV)

Through my mom's life, I saw this promise of God fulfilled. She followed God with her whole heart, living according to His teaching. She didn't question His goodness because of pain, but she pressed into deeper faith. I saw firsthand God's outpouring of the "oil of joy" in my mom's life.

The "oil of joy" she received as a blessing from God overflowed to me that day as I sat at her bedside. In the months that have passed since my mom left this earth and was received into the glory of heaven, God has taken my tears of oil that began three years ago in sorrow and transformed them into the oil of joy!

I am learning that having joy doesn't mean an absence of pain. Joy doesn't ignore the reality of loss. Joy co-exists with pain because it is based on a future hope, not the present circumstances.

I am learning that joy's sign isn't bubbling-over laughter and the omission of hurt. Instead, it is displayed by a posture and gratitude that looks beyond the rushing current, tumultuous waves, and storms of life. Despite all that may be present around me, my vision is set on the hope of what is to come, the fulfillment of God's promise. My eyes are set on the clear blue skies up ahead.

My mom made a choice that we each must make. Will we allow the mountain ahead to tell us how small we are or how big our God is? Will we fixate on the depravity of this world or the abundance of God's presence?

As Jesus taught the disciples to pray, He said, *Your kingdom come, Your will be done, on earth as it is in heaven."* (Matthew 6:10 NIV)

Heaven on earth looks like the radiance of peace and joy—the oil of joy poured out on God's people—if we allow Him to comfort us in such a way.

I hope that no matter what you are facing, this picture of Jesus pouring out His comforting, anointing oil of joy gives you hope that He can and will do the same for you. I pray that the story of my mom's joy, even in the hardest and darkest of her days, inspires you to look to God as your source of hope, peace, comfort, and joy.

As you wrap up this reading and go about your day, I pray that you arise changed. Ask God to help you to see that He is using every tear for your good. He may not show you how He will use them or tell you why, but He will reassure you, letting you know that He is using every hurt and every heartache for your good.

I pray that it challenged you to see joy in a new light and know that joy is possible amid the pain you have been walking in. I pray that you are encouraged to surrender to the loving arms of Jesus, where you will find comfort, hope, peace, and love like no other can give.

Joy in Who He Is

The joy of the Lord is your strength. (Nehemiah 8:10 ESV)

How can we not believe that the God of the universe gives us joy? The joy that makes us get up in the mornings. The joy we exude when we are with the people we love the most. The joy when we watch little children open gifts on Christmas morning. This pure and authentic joy could only be from God. This is who He is. Psalm 16:11 says, *You make known to me the path of life; in your presence, there is fullness of joy; at your right hand are pleasures forevermore.* (ESV)

Have you ever just been so happy and ready to conquer the day? Even when life is not going as you expected? This is the joy of the Lord. This is who He says He is. God is joy personified.

When we walk through suffering knowing who God is, we are brought to a deeper intimacy with Him as we fall deeper in love. The joy of the Lord makes us stronger, allowing us to walk into any situation, look through different lenses, and recognize that God is there and He will never leave us alone. When we step out in faith, He meets us right where we are, confirming we are doing what He has called us to do and making our joy within explode. Joy is always available to us because God is always with us, and He keeps His promises to our hearts.

Joy keeps us alive in Christ. To think of all that God has done for us blows my mind! He sent His only Son to die for us, turning our brokenness into joy. He provides and cares for us, telling us not to worry—so we can flourish joyfully. He calls us to surrender as He stands ready to fill us with His joyful presence and every essence of who He is. *This* is our God.

Perhaps there have been times you have questioned the joy of the Lord. You may, even now, be going through a season of wondering where God is. As daughters of the King, we are called to process our many emotions in God's presence. When we do process—through praying, reading scripture, writing, or even talking with a friend—if we allow God to be part of the conversation, He quickly reminds us that even in our grief, tears, and moans, He is always there and in control. God never leaves our side, even when we are in the middle of a mess. Trusting God's provision and presence allows us to walk through any circumstance secure in His joy, allowing peace to reside in our hearts even in the hardest seasons.

God is so faithful! That is who He is. Open your eyes to Him in obedience. Ask Him to reveal Himself and all His characteristics. Our God is never changing. He is consistent, loving, and a father to the fatherless. He is a mender of the brokenhearted and He is the lover of our souls. Our Lord is the drink that never runs dry and the comforter in our pain.

And because He is all this, God is our ultimate joy giver. Give Him permission today to shower you with the joy He longs to pour out on you—the joy that can only come from Him. Let down your guard and let the worries of the world slip off your shoulders as you soak in the joy of who our Lord is!

. . . .

Elaine Nasworthy

Elaine is a woman who has worn many hats in her lifetime. A wife, mother, grandmother, teacher, and friend. She and her husband, Elbert, are both fifth-generation Floridians, a rare accomplishment these days. He was her middle school sweetheart, and they have been married for over 50 years. She grew up on a dairy farm east of Tampa. At the age of 10, she went to Camp Gilead Bible Camp and accepted Christ as her Savior.

Her husband recently retired as senior pastor of a local church. She is currently serving with him as he ministers as an interim pastor in Florida. She is also retired after being a schoolteacher in both public and private Christian schools.

Elaine's greatest accomplishments are being a wife, mother, and grandmother. Her daughter is a nurse, and her son is a firefighter. She is also the proud grandmother to one grandson and two granddaughters.

Her passion is teaching children and encouraging those who work in children's ministries.

Down-in-My-Heart Joy
by Elaine Nasworthy

Is there a difference between being happy and being joyful? We tend to equate the two words. You know English is a funny language. We sometimes use different words to give the same message. And at times, we ignore the nuances of the individual words, using them interchangeably in error.

The Merriam-Webster Dictionary definition of *happiness* is the "state of well-being; a pleasurable or satisfying experience." The definition of the word *rejoice,* related to the word *joy,* is "to feel great delight; to be glad."

Can we be joyful without being happy? Can we "feel delight" without being in a "state of well-being"? Through my life, and through one particular trying circumstance, I realized my heart *can* be rooted in joy, despite what is thrown at me.

For many years I was a preschool/kindergarten teacher in private Christian schools. I used music during my day with the children to instill in them the truths of God's Word and their self-esteem. Ongoingly, one of the children's favorite songs caused them to gleefully raise their voices, sharing that they had the joy of the Lord. Where? Down in their hearts!

I tried to teach them that joy does not equal happiness, that although some days they were not happy, they could always have joy. Joy is down in their heart to stay.

In the Bible, James says in James 1:2-3 that we should, *consider it a great joy, my brothers, and sisters, whenever you experience various trials, because you know that the testing of your faith produces endurance.* (CSB) Another version translates it this way: *Count it all joy, my brothers, when you meet trials of various kinds, for you know that the testing of your faith produces steadfastness.* (ESV)

So where does that leave the believer who is facing insurmountable trials? Where is that joy we are supposed to have? I am sure many of us have those questions. Some days we just don't feel happy, much less joyful. And isn't that to be expected? After all, look at what is happening in the world: personal issues with health and marriages; difficulties with children, addictions, finances, and employment; and even more overarching problems that affect us on a national or worldwide level.

As a pastor's wife (now retired), I have ministered to many people burdened with heavy issues. When given the opportunity to counsel them, I always cover their salvation first, and then we delve into their problems. Often, individuals are in such spiritual warfare that they see no way of escape. They have no happiness, and they feel that their joy is gone. Women have told me, "But you don't know what I am going through. You're a pastor's wife." While that may be true of a specific situation, I reiterate that no one has led a perfect life. Everyone has struggles. I may not be able to sympathize with an exact situation, but I can certainly empathize with a lack of joy. One of Satan's greatest tools against believers is discouragement, which he tries to use to rob us of our joy. We are in a battle! But I will assure them that Satan cannot steal our salvation, and if you hold close to God, Satan cannot rob you of your joy.

A very distraught young woman I met with told me she had accepted Christ as her Savior some years before but was now not happy. She was afraid because she had made some bad choices. After processing with God, she finally realized that her joy was not dependent on those circumstances or her happiness but was deeply rooted in who she was in Christ. She made the decision to rededicate her life to the Lord and begin trusting Him again. She committed to reading her Bible, going to church, and removing herself from the situations and people Satan was using to pull her away from the very essence of who she was—a child of the King.

Let me go back to my story. My wisdom on joy and happiness was not easily earned but was a tough lesson taught to me many years ago. Let me share with you my story in hopes that God will speak to you through it.

We were only nineteen when I married my husband, Thumper, in 1971. (Just a clarification: his name is Elbert, but when he was born, his family nicknamed him Thumper. Professionally, he is Elbert.) My husband went to school full-time while I worked. Initially, we felt God leading us into full-time ministry, but God's timing was different from ours. Like so many people in the Bible, we had some growing up to do. And God had some lessons to teach us.

After graduating college, my husband went to work in his family's business. We started our family, and God blessed us with two children.

Our firstborn was a girl we named Lacey.

After a few years, we wanted to add to our family, but my next pregnancy ended in a miscarriage. Then I had some problems with fertility. Through a lot of testing, I got pregnant again. Another miscarriage. Were we happy with these circumstances? No. But we had the indescribable "joy of the Lord." He was our strength. Then surprisingly, I got pregnant. Were we apprehensive? You bet. In fact, we didn't tell anyone about the pregnancy until I was three months along and beginning to get the bump.

Finally, we were blessed with Erik, our baby boy, born in 1980.

Our lives were pretty good. We were actively involved in a wonderful church, and I was a stay-at-home mom of two children, always working hard to keep the kids busy. I had no real stress. We had a good marriage, good kids, good church, good home, good health, and good finances. No problems. I was happy! What could possibly go wrong?

Let me just set the stage. Then came 1982. We lived in a rural area in Brandon, Florida, just east of Tampa, in an older ranch-style home built in the 1960s. It had terrazzo floors, a paneled family room, a fireplace, and sliding glass doors. The kitchen had some unique qualities, including a state-of-the-art stove called a Flair. The burners on the stove pulled out like a drawer, very low to the floor. The novelty was that it was a full-size cooking top that "disappears at a touch."

Lacey, then six, was a bundle of joy—she was smart and energetic. Erik, 18 months old, was one of those kids who could occupy himself with the simplest items. When he got a gift, he was entranced with the box it came in; he played endlessly with the Tupperware in the kitchen cabinets and was always eager to help with tasks around the house.

Summers were hot, the humidity was high, and I did everything to keep the kids busy. It was a beautiful Friday—one of those hot, humid Florida days. July 4th was that Sunday, and we had planned to go to the beach for the weekend. Thumper was going to play golf. That morning, I took the kids to the park, something we regularly did. Yes, I was the perfect mother. But I also had an ulterior motive. I would take them so they could run off some of their energy, and then we would go home and take naps. Sometimes we took a picnic, but I didn't pack a lunch on this day. They ran, swung on the swings, played catch, and ran some more. As I began to see they were slowing down and getting hungry, we loaded up and went home for lunch and naps before our weekend away.

The children were in the kitchen with me as I was preparing lunch. I had pulled out the burners on the Flair and put some eggs in a pot of water to boil. I turned my back for a brief second, and when I turned back, I saw Erik with the pot lid in his hand. As he reached to put the lid on the boiling pot of water, I yelled. When I did, the lid was almost on the pot; Erik jerked his hand and caught the pot with the lid, pulling the boiling water onto his body. The scalding water landed between his nipples and his waist, puddling on the top of his diaper.

I screamed for Lacey to go to the bathroom to get a towel as I pulled off his diaper. I could already see the skin peeling off his little body. I wet the towel with cold water and wrapped it around his middle area. The doctors said that this probably prevented his burns from being worse.

Times were a lot different in 1982. There was no 911, no fire stations nearby, and no cell phones. Praise the Lord, we did have a relatively new hospital about five miles away.

I ushered Lacey to the front seat of the car as I picked up Erik, still wrapped with the wet towel, and then put him on Lacey's lap. I remember looking over at the two of them—she was in total control, carefully and securely holding him. I really don't remember him screaming, but I'm sure he did. Sometimes painful memories are a fog in our memory banks.

We got to the hospital. I quickly parked and ran in carrying Erik, with Lacey right on our heels. I don't remember much of what happened next. I do remember calling my husband's office and telling the person who answered that they needed to find him. Thumper was a salesman and traveled around the area. Again, there were no cell phones. I got in touch with my mother, and she came and picked up Lacey so she wouldn't have to sit in that waiting room scared to death.

The nurses and doctors began to work on Erik. First, they had to clean the burn. I again don't remember much about the procedure. Thumper finally arrived, and we met with the doctors who told us we could take Erik home (really?) and take him to his pediatrician the next day. It was a long night. We put Erik in our bed and took turns sleeping on the couch.

The next day we took Erik to the pediatrician's office. When we arrived, both our regular pediatricians were off for the weekend, so we saw a new doctor. When she unwrapped the bandage, you could tell she was stunned. She told us that he had second-degree burns on his chest and third-degree burns on his lower abdomen. His diaper had helped protect him from being burned in his genital area. She also said that he would need to see a surgeon and that it would be a long, arduous healing process.

You know, our God is an awesome God. We "just happened" to know a surgeon, Dr. David Worthington, right there in our community. He and his family went to church with us, so we called and got an immediate appointment.

David, the surgeon, unwrapped the bandage. We could see the somber look on his face. He was a very quiet man, but we could tell that what he had to share with us was grueling, even for an experienced surgeon.

David reiterated that Erik did indeed have second and third-degree burns on 30% of his body. He explained to us the severity of those burns, stating that third-degree burns go through the first two layers of skin and into the third and lowest layer of the skin. The only good thing about third-degree burns is that there is no pain in that area because the epidermis and hair follicles are destroyed. He said that individuals with burns like Erik's need to be hospitalized as they are susceptible to infections and need fluid resuscitation administered intravenously. Additionally, Erik's healing process required daily debriding of the dead skin (I will go into that later) and bathing in a special tub. David also said that Erik would need multiple skin grafts as he grew, but despite that, he would still have a very serious scar. Then he said, jokingly, that Erik would not have a hairy chest.

Thumper and I sat and looked at each other, stunned. Then Thumper said, "Why can't we do all of that at home?"

David again explained the intensity of caring for a burn victim.

We adamantly said that we could take care of our baby at home. David finally relented, saying that if he did not know us, he would not agree to our idea. He then gave us explicit instructions for Erik's care and told us we were to call him if we saw any changes. David gave us a trial run until Friday, stating that it was likely Erik would have to be hospitalized at that point. We went home with our baby boy—and our list.

We were scared to death. How would we handle this? Neither one of us had any medical experience. But we serve a mighty God. We immediately called our pastor, deacons, and Sunday school teacher, who began to have a special prayer for us.

Were we happy? Of course not.

Did we have joy? Not at the time, but we had the peace of God.

Nehemiah 8:10 says, *the joy of the LORD is your strength.* (CSB) The Lord was our strength.

Living in a small community has great advantages sometimes. Thumper went to our local pharmacist, John, at Bill's Prescription with the list of items necessary to care for Erik: sterile gauze pads, sterile gauze to wrap his body, betadine to debride his skin, and sterile washcloths to scrub him. Yes,

I said scrub. We also had a prescription for silver sulfadiazine, or Silvadene, the topical antibiotic used in full-thickness burns to prevent infection. Unfortunately, our health insurance didn't cover these items, which were very expensive. But Erik needed these supplies, and we would do anything to take care of our baby.

Twice a day, we needed to debride Erik. We sterilized the bathtub, unwrapped the bandages, and carefully put him into the warm water. We poured the betadine on the wound and used soft, sterilized washcloths to remove the dead skin. It was indescribable what we had to do to our baby, but with a lot of prayer, God gave us strength. Thumper came home every day so we could go through this excruciating process—it was a two-person job. Again, family, church, and community were so important to us. Thumper's parents were on a long trip, and we were unable to contact them. But his grandparents were right beside us, helping with whatever we needed. In fact, they bought us enough sterile washcloths for us to have an abundant inventory. My mother took care of Lacey, and fellow church members provided all our meals. Our daily needs were met.

As Friday approached, we were nervous wrecks. But we knew there were no serious visible changes in Erik's wound, and we were prayed up. Our church family was praying, and our close family was praying. I will never forget that drive to David's office. There was a county park close by, and Thumper drove to the park and pulled into the parking lot under the trees. We had Erik in the front seat with us. We each put our arms around him and prayed to our God who heals. It was the most powerful prayer session that I have ever experienced. We were ready.

We went into the examination room. David entered and began to unwrap the bandages. In his quiet professional demeanor, he began to examine Erik's wound. He finally stopped and looked up at us with tears in his eyes. We did not know what to expect him to say. He looked each of us in the eyes and said that he never, in all his years treating burn victims, had seen anyone with a burn as severe as Erik's heal as quickly as he had.

What? Were we hearing him correctly? Yes, we were. Our God healed our baby boy. Was the process over? No. But the worst was over. We left that office that day with a joy that was indescribable.

There were so many blessings God showered us with throughout our ordeal. Although we had to continue the debriding process for weeks, God provided financially through our local pharmacist, John. He saw how much we were spending on the bandages and other supplies for the wound treatment, so he arranged for us to purchase the bandages directly from the wholesaler and sold us the prescription at his cost.

Erik began to heal. I don't remember how long it took, but he never spent a day in the hospital, and to this day, he has never had a skin graft. In fact, he even has a hairy chest! And he is now a firefighter, helping others in their most terrifying moments.

And the hospital that first cared for Erik, which was only five miles away? It had been built on land donated by a group of investors, including my father-in-law. We never know how God will use our obedience to bless others—even those we love.

And big sister Lacey? As a registered nurse, she spends her time caring for others—in the same hospital that treated Erik. Amazing, huh?

God taught us many lessons throughout this whole process. We learned how to pray, how to lean on others, how to prioritize our needs, and how to trust God in "all circumstances." And we learned that it is possible to have joy, even in the middle of the worst days. Joy is a gift from God that only He can offer.

We gain joy as we grasp the reality that we are truly safe and cared for by Him, despite our circumstances.

Were we *happy* as we cared for our hurting baby boy? Absolutely not.

But we had *joy*—down in our hearts.

Joy in His Goodness

God is so good; He demonstrates His goodness through His actions toward us. And His first action is also the most important: that is His love for us. God's love is great and ever-abounding. We can see evidence of God's goodness the moment we open our eyes each day. His love shines like joy through our windows. You are alive to see daylight because of the goodness of God.

The goodness of God is one of His attributes and a description of His very essence. Throughout God's Word, the Bible, we can see that God is inherently good.

> *Taste and see that the Lord is good; blessed is the one who takes refuge in him.* (Psalm 34:8 NIV)

God is the foundation of everything good. It did not take any other source to make Him good; goodness is His character. We can try to do honorable deeds or have the privilege of being provided an excellent upbringing that allows us to become an individual of high standards, but if we have any goodness in us, we can be assured that it comes from God!

God's goodness provides for us and gives us a model to follow. We, in our flesh, strive to do good things, but true goodness only resides in and by the power of God. As the psalmist says of God, You are good, and what you do is good; teach me your decrees. (Psalm 119:68 NIV)

> *Every good and perfect gift is from above, coming down from the Father of the heavenly lights, who does not change like shifting shadows.* (James 1:17 NIV)

We must also realize that good things for us do not always show up as happy or fun experiences. Sometimes good can come masked as adversity or hardships. Please understand that God, in His goodness, can use difficulties for good. He communicates this to us in Romans 8:28, *And we know that in all things God works for the good of those who love him, who have been called according to his purpose.* (NIV)

The deeper we know God, the more we understand that He will never change and the more we can rejoice that His goodness will always remain. Psalm 52:1 says, *The goodness of God endureth continually.* (KJV) We can find joy in knowing God will always be good. God's character does not change. By His goodness, God provided salvation through His Son. He supplied a need for us out of the goodness of who He is. That need is a gift that offers salvation for all humankind who choose to accept His good gift. Our goal should be to carry the joy of His goodness to others every day so that they, too, may know the joy of salvation and the goodness of God!

Ruby Tucker

Ruby Tucker has held many titles, including Advertising/Sales Promotion Director, Interior Decorator, Seamstress, Electronics Assembler/Tester, Waitress, and Caregiver. She was born in Tennessee in 1941, moved to Ohio at the age of 10, and then to South Florida in 1977 at the age of 36. She accepted Jesus Christ as her Lord and Savior at the age of 12, walked away from Him at the age of 19, and came back to Him at the age of 36. She loves to sing in her church choir and be in Bible study.

Ruby performed and sang in a megachurch Christmas pageant for 11 years in South Florida. The pageant was televised worldwide and won several Emmys.

For ten years, she performed and sang in a traveling minimalist play founded by the late Travis Johnson of Revelation Ministries. They performed in churches, prisons, and holding facilities for immigrants throughout South Florida and also traveled to Israel, England, Russia, and Ukraine, often presenting in the local language. Ruby witnessed many miracles while serving with Revelation Ministries and saw hundreds accept Jesus Christ as their Lord and Savior.

Ruby is a friend to many, an aunt to four children, a great-aunt to six children, and a great-great-aunt to 12 children.

Fishing With Bagels, Catching HIS Joy

by Ruby Tucker

Life was proceeding normally for this single gal living in South Florida. I was so excited because I had just been presented with a marvelous opportunity to live on the beach for a week—TOTALLY FREE! Then suddenly, without warning, my life changed. I had a stroke. As I was in the ER (emergency room) waiting to be transported to the ICU (intensive care unit), I remembered Psalm 23:4 *Even though I walk through the valley of the shadow of death, I will fear no evil, for You are with me; Your rod and Your staff, they comfort me.* (ESV) Despite my circumstance, God's promise to me cut through the gloom, giving me peace.

I had to claim that same verse again just ten days later when I suffered another stroke, this one even worse than the first. My second stroke left me unable to walk, talk, or write, but GOD was with me! Deuteronomy 31:6 says, *Be strong and courageous. Do not be afraid or terrified because of them, for the LORD your God goes with you; He will never leave you nor forsake you.* (NIV) Holding onto that verse gave me peace, reminding me I was in God's hands.

But my trials were still not finished. Two days later, I had a brain aneurysm that required surgery.

Depression or sadness could have reared their ugly heads, for it was certain that I would not EVER be the same again. But they didn't. Because my GOD said in Nehemiah 8:10, *Do not grieve, for the joy of the LORD is your strength.* (NIV)

I have JOY because I know what GOD has brought me through. So what is there to be sad about? No matter what happens, you can have that same peace and JOY…if you believe! I hope my story will inspire you.

By the way, the title of this chapter, "Fishing With Bagels," really happened! It was simply one step in my journey of joy, brought to me in unexpected ways.

· · · · · · · · · · · · · · · · · · ·

My story began on a Saturday.

Some friends had generously offered me the opportunity to stay at their timeshare on the beach for a week. To say I was excited was an understatement, but when the time came, I just didn't feel like driving the short distance to get there, so I stayed home.

On Sunday, I talked myself into getting groceries and headed to the beach timeshare, settling in for my stay.

After work on Monday, I took the scenic route back to my temporary beach home, where I fixed supper. Then, as I sat on the beautiful sofa, I proceeded to drop my bowl of spaghetti all over the couch, me, and the floor. But instead of jumping up to clean the mess, I just sat there. Later, I discovered I was having TIA's (transient ischemic attacks). The rest of the week went slowly and uneventfully, but Friday was a different story.

On Friday, Jo Ann, the wife of the timeshare owner, came to my work to pick up the keys. She took one look at me, heard me speak, and said I didn't look or sound like myself. She got on the phone immediately with my doctor's office and was told the nurse would call back. When the nurse called, she told me to hang up and dial 911, which, of course, I did not do. Instead, I asked Jo Ann to take me to the nearest ER. I thought it strange when they called me back first, even though the waiting room was full of people. After I had an x-ray and MRI, the medical staff began buzzing all around me, telling me I was having a major stroke.

While I was waiting to go to the ICU, Jo Ann called everybody. I knew I was in deep trouble and recognized I had no choice but to walk this personal journey God had set me on. It was at that moment Psalm 23:4 came to me, *Yea, though I walk through the valley of the shadow of death, I will fear no evil: for Thou art with me; Thy rod and Thy staff they comfort me.* (KJV) I was not alone; God was with me.

After being in the ICU for several days, I was moved to another floor for rehab. Eric, a good friend and associate pastor at the church I formerly attended, came to see me. He and his wife were on their way home from a few days in the Florida Keys, and he had wanted to stop in to see how I was doing. Eric visited and prayed with me. The next day I was transported to a rehabilitation facility. Every nurse and aide who came into my room that week either prayed or spoke a Bible verse over me. Blessings and prayers flooded my spirit, reminding me who was in control.

I eventually returned home to my condominium to recover, with an order to return to the doctor's office for a follow-up, including a reading of my MRI. On the day of my appointment, the neurosurgeon was called into emergency surgery. The nurse let me know every hour that the doctor was still in surgery, and finally, at 9 pm, she called saying the doctor had read my MRI and brain scan reports, and I was to be at his office at 3:00 pm the next day, Tuesday, July 17. I knew that I was in deep trouble.

That next day, my friend Charlotte came to see me. I had a headache that was the world's worst—never before had I experienced pain like that. NEVER. I couldn't even stand or walk straight. Charlotte said, "Ruby, whatever you do, don't throw up." But I told Charlotte I was going to do just that. She got a basin. She was so sweet. And then she cleaned up my mess. I have the world's greatest friends.

I knew I had to shower before my other friends, Gwen and Alyce, arrived to take me to my appointment. I made it to the shower but could only manage to sit on the side of the tub and take a spit bath. When we arrived at the doctor's office for the appointment, the doctor told me I was having a second stroke, this time with a brain aneurysm. I was to be admitted immediately. He said to go through the emergency room because it would be faster. Gwen and Alyce graciously wheeled me there. A child in the waiting room was crying loudly, so I asked my friends to take me outside because I just couldn't tolerate the noise, but at that moment, the attendant admitted me. I was taken to a room where a male nurse gave me a shot of codeine, to which I had a horrible reaction. I sat straight up in bed, trembling and feeling like I was going to die, and I told the nurse never to give me that again. I felt sorry for the nurse and apologized.

The next day 25 or 30 of my wonderful, precious friends surrounded my bed and prayed for me. As Jo Ann wrote down my last wishes, a young pastor friend, Stephen, leaned down and said, "Ruby Tucker, you are NOT going to die." And I didn't.

Quickly, I was scheduled for surgery. As I was being rolled into the operating room, some nurses wished my doctor a happy birthday. I told him my birthday was a day after his, and he got down in my face and said, "Ruby, I'm going to give you the best birthday present you ever had." And he did.

In recovery after the surgery, the doctor told me he wasn't the only person in the operating room—when he opened my cerebellum, a blood clot bigger than a golf ball just rolled into his hands. I was joyfully reminded that God is my true healer.

On my birthday, July 20, 2001, I was moved from ICU. There I was in the hospital with a huge bandage on my head when my friends, led by Richard and Barbara, had a birthday party for me. Joy despite the turmoil.

Next, I was taken to North Broward Hospital for six weeks of rehab. My room had a big window to look out at the sky. God continued to be with me as He showed me a sign in every cloud that went by—an angel, a harp, a choir, or something else. Then, toward the end of my time in rehab, three gentlemen and I were taken to Crystal Lake to fish. We fished from the boardwalk with bagels. The bagels fell off the hooks as soon as they hit the water, but we didn't care. We were free for an hour or so. Such unexpected JOY, because we had HIS JOY! Sometimes God's joy finds us in the most unusual circumstances!

When I returned home from rehab, my friends Greg and Mary Jane brought food and ate with me. It was a real treat. My friends Jo Ann, Debbie, and Risé took turns coming over every weekday after work. Debbie, my hairdresser, introduced me to hazelnut coffee. I'm hooked on it to this day! Jo Ann and Risé were massage therapists, and they accompanied me with my walker to my condo pool, helped me get into the pool, and walked me back and forth in the shallow end to strengthen my legs. It sure did help. Today, I walk as well as I do because of the good LORD and my friends. God provided what I needed through my friends, who each gave me exactly what they were able to—which was exactly what I needed to recover well and experience joy in the arduous process.

My sister Carolyn and my brother Larry are also stroke survivors. Carolyn traveled from Phoenix to see how I was doing and assist me with appointments. She and my best friend Diana brought me a Bushie, a multicolored clown wig, to cover my shaved head. Then they took me to dinner all dolled up. We got a lot of questionable looks and giggles. What a joyful time we had.

The devil must have sensed our joy, and he doesn't give up easily! Our fun times ended when we got home, opened the kitchen door, and water poured out all over our feet. My kitchen was dripping wet, including everything in the cabinets. The water had come from the condo above mine. It was not a pretty sight, and it took a lot of work to get it cleaned. But even that did not stop my joy. God promises to walk through the fire with His children. Take it from me—He will also walk through a soaking-wet kitchen with us, even after brain surgery.

Next, God showed me that no problem is too big for Him—He always provides. God sent Carolyn to help me fill out paperwork for much-needed food stamps, then Gwen and her husband Nick came over to make sure I had all the necessary papers, and the next day Gwen took me to the appointment. We just knew I would be approved, so we were all shocked when my request was denied. I was told that I had too much money. Gwen was nearly in tears, but the lack of food stamps didn't steal my JOY! I knew God had this covered.

My friend Barbara took me to the Social Security Office for another appointment. To our surprise and thankfulness, I was approved but would have to wait seven months for the payments to be issued. That seven-month wait gave me ample time to see God bring the biggest miracle of all—His provision for living seven months with no money. My mortgage was paid, my electric bill was paid, and food was brought to me—all by friends and acquaintances. Donna and Kathy brought bags of food every Saturday from the church food bank. And Alyce prepared delicious meals for me. God brought His community together in ways I couldn't have begun to imagine.

It was five years before the doctors gave me permission to drive and one more year before I got a car. My friend Rosemary came over with a car and, handing me the keys, said, "It's yours."

Unbelievable! It was another miracle.

Through all these trials and tribulations, I remained full of joy. I know this was and is because the joy I experienced was God's! God didn't take me through strokes, a broken brain aneurysm, brain surgery, and many other things so that I could put Him in a closet. He wants me to tell others about what He has done. And He knows He can trust me to do just that. Besides, I say God doesn't want me to live full-time in His kingdom yet. So He has left me here, saying, "I am not ready for her now!"

Still, God has provided me with joy unspeakable now, and I will have eternal joy unspeakable when my final breath on this earth comes. Whenever God decides is the right time.

Life's struggles are like a hurricane—we don't know where it's coming ashore or how big and strong it will be. So we have to be prepared. As we journey through life, we have no idea what may come at us at any given moment—maybe a stroke or cancer, and at some point, even death itself. Do you know where you are going when you die? You CAN be prepared. You can have JOY for life's journey, even when death is imminent, if you have Jesus! If you know where you are going when you die, the JOY of the Lord will carry you through all that life can throw your way.

Do you know Him? Accept Jesus today. You can know HIS JOY. There is nothing like it! Be prepared! JESUS will give you JOY UNSPEAKABLE! Accept Him today. I would not have made it if it weren't for Jesus, my Savior. My life was and is in His hands! Deuteronomy 31:6 NIV says, *"He will never leave you nor forsake you."* EVER! All you have to do is believe in Him, trust Him and accept Him as your Lord and Savior.

And be ready for Him to bless you in the unexpected. Who knows, He may even give you a chance to fish with bagels!

God bless you.

JOY IN SICKNESS & IN HEALTH

When my husband and I took our wedding vows over 40 years ago, one of our vows was to love each other "in sickness and in health." We were so young, starry-eyed, and in love that we never thought we would actually endure health issues. We have since experienced many illnesses and health challenges. With God's help, we each care for the other because of our commitment, vows, and love.

As much as my husband and I love and help each other, God's love and provision are so much greater—they are unfathomable. God is beside us, comforting and carrying us through health issues. And He continues to be our sustainer, strengthening both of us. The Lord provides for us in our time of need, both directly and through the help of other brothers and sisters in Christ. His care and comfort have taught us to relate to, care for, and comfort others when they experience similar challenges. *He comforts us in all our troubles so that we can comfort others. When they are troubled, we will be able to give them the same comfort God has given us.* (2 Corinthians 1:4 NLT)

When we are weak, He is strong. Our weakness, whether due to sickness or hardships, allows others to see God working in and through our lives, pointing as a testimony directly to Him. God gets all the glory! The apostle Paul spoke about having a thorn in his side. He pleaded with the Lord three times to take it away from him, but the Lord said to him, *"My grace is sufficient for you, for my power is made perfect in weakness."* (2 Corinthians 12:9 NIV) After that, Paul boasted all the more gladly about his weaknesses and difficulties, telling others he couldn't continue without the power of Christ in him.

Did you know that joy can help improve your health? It can help you be less worried and anxious, thereby lowering your stress, blood pressure, and the risk of a heart attack. Wow! That's a great side benefit of having joy!

When we endure sickness—or any trial, for that matter—with joy, hope, and peace, we attract the curiosity of others who will want what we have. God uses everything for His glory, and our humble testimony of why we have such joy, hope, and peace during our troubles and illnesses points others to the Lord. The joy of the Lord truly is our strength.

Yes, even Christians suffer illness—both temporary and terminal. Some people receive physical healing while still on this earth, for God's glory; others receive complete healing with a new body on the other side of eternity, also for His Glory. Either way, we are healed. We can endure these afflictions because we have joy, hope, and peace, knowing that sooner or later, we will have a new body, free from any sickness and health problems. Now that's something to be joyful about!

. . . .

Sandra Fincher Porter

Sandra Fincher Porter, from Jonesboro, Georgia, is a Christian, a pastor's wife, mother, and grandmother. She has three daughters and five grandchildren, ranging in age from 15 to 3 years old, who bring her great joy. Knowing grandchildren are a gift from God, Sandra knows she is blessed to live close to hers.

Sandra takes care of the kitchen of her church, helping prepare Wednesday night dinners and all things kitchen/food related. She also helps in the nursery, which she especially enjoys as her youngest daughter and family attend the same church, so she gets to see these babies at church on Wednesdays and Sundays.

Sandra helped found Oasis Pregnancy Care Centers in 2009 and has served on the board as President of the Board of Directors since. Oasis Pregnancy Care Center's purpose is to help women of all ages choose life rather than abortion for their baby and to educate them on life choices as they show them the love of Jesus.

Sandra retired from Delta Airlines in 2009 after 33 years. When asked if she is enjoying her retirement, Sandra says she is busier than she has ever been and absolutely loves it! She is blessed beyond measure! God is Amazing!

Finding Joy Unspeakable in the Midst of a Tragedy

by Sandra Fincher Porter

On Saturday, March 5, 2005, I began an unforgettable, painful journey. Yet through it, God showed me clearly that He can provide *Joy Unspeakable* in the midst of a tragedy.

First, I learned that God provides joy and comfort through His people.

I was at work for Northwest Airlines in our Tampa office when I received a call from a number I didn't recognize. Afraid of what I might hear, I answered. An emergency room doctor in Atlanta said my husband of 20 years, Frank, was killed that morning after an accident while trimming a tree from the top of a ladder.

I don't even know how I responded.

Immediately, my co-workers jumped into action. A sweet friend took my hands and prayed with me as others encircled me. Then they gathered my things, arranged air transportation to Atlanta, and located our daughter Jennifer.

Jennifer, 16 years old, was part of a study group at her teacher's home. I told the teacher over the phone what happened and asked her to tell Jennifer to come home immediately because we needed to go to Atlanta. In hindsight, I should have left off the Atlanta part because she figured out what had probably happened.

A friend drove me home while I made phone calls. I called my pastor, who prayed with me and said he would notify our church family. Then I prepared to call Frank's children. Frank was 20 years older than me, so his kids were adults. I was relieved to learn Frank's boss had already called them personally. Next, I called Frank's twin sister, who, of course, was devastated. Next, I called my family and my lifelong best friend, Debbie.

I arrived home with my mind spinning, but friends from church were already there to help. There was so much to do: important papers to find and clothes to pack for the trip and for the funeral. I began making a list. When Jennifer got home, we cried and somehow got our things packed. Then, my friend took us to the airport, waiting with us to be sure we were smoothly on our way.

> *I can do all things through Christ who strengthens me.* (Philippians 4:13 NKJV)

Then I learned God provides joy in tragedy through His orchestration of events.

We had not seen Frank for three months, since just before Christmas. He was working in Atlanta while Jennifer and I were busy in Tampa. We kept trying to get together, but the weather would not agree, and our schedules did not work out to make a trip. So instead, we talked on the phone as often as possible.

Frank was dependable and loved serving others. He worked at the church as a custodian, taking great pride in his job—always doing his best without attracting attention to himself. He also loved taking care of our house and the yard and even helping others with their homes. At 69 years old, he could outwork a man half his age.

We could see God's grace at work in several ways. First, the fact that Frank died doing something he loved, yardwork, was comforting. Secondly, we also felt God's mercy in allowing him to die instantly. Frank was not in prolonged pain, and we didn't have to agonize over any decisions regarding life support. Third, Frank had just spent the previous weekend with his three older children, two grandchildren, and a great-granddaughter, and had a wonderful time.

We were in shock, of course, but we knew Frank was in heaven.

> *And we know that all things work together for good to those who love God, to those who are called according to His purpose.* (Romans 8:28 NKJV)

We got to Atlanta later that evening. Frank's oldest son and his wife picked us up at the airport. When we arrived at our house around 11 pm, the tree limb and the ladder were still in the front yard. That was very difficult to see.

My brother was there waiting for us, along with Debbie, so we were surrounded by family.

When we entered the house, it was spotless except for the plate and coffee cup from Frank's breakfast in the sink. Frank had taken care of the bills and the mail the night before. How do I know? The trash can and folding TV table were sitting next to the rocking chair in front of the TV. That scene was very comforting to me. Frank had read the mail and paid the bills the night before. He was always taking care of us.

There was something else, a sweet surprise for Jennifer and me. Frank had told me on the phone he had gotten us both a birthday present. Jennifer's birthday is February 3, and mine is June 29. He would not tell me what the presents were. When we walked in that night, there were two new recliners in the den placed in front of each other as if in a theater, with his very old, worn-out recliner that only he could sit in because the footrest would not close was in the back row. We all laughed!

After many tears, hugs, and stories of Frank, my brother, my stepson, and his wife went home. My best friend Debbie was prepared to be there as long as she was needed. That's what best friends do, right?! Needless to say, we stayed up talking, crying, and reminiscing for a while. It was very sweet.

In the morning, as Jennifer and I were getting ready for church, we heard noises out front. We looked out the window to see several teens from church hand-sawing the huge tree limb, cleaning up the debris, and hauling away everything, including the ladder. What a blessing!

When we arrived at church, friends and church members surrounded us. In the service, the pastor announced Frank's death first. Then, at prayer time, Jennifer and I went to pray on the altar steps. Soon, nearly all of the church members were there praying with us!

> *Let us therefore come boldly to the throne of grace, that we may obtain mercy and find grace to help in time of need.* (Hebrews 4:16 NKJV)

Shortly after we got home from church, the doorbell rang. The daughter of one of my co-workers in Tampa was standing there with a meal for us. Her mother had called and told her, "You have to bring lunch to them today." We were blessed by someone in Tampa through her daughter, who lives in Atlanta. That, my sweet friends, is God's hand at work!

When looking for clothes for Frank to be buried in, I went into our closet, opened the door, and saw Frank's side of the closet was very tidy. His clothes were neatly hung with shirts, then pants, then work-type clothes. But there was one amazing thing! Three hangers were between the shirts and the pants, separated from the other clothes. His favorite blue dress shirt, tie, dress pants, and his favorite suit coat were all hanging together, separate from the rest of the clothes. It was as if he needed me to know these were the clothes he wanted to be buried in.

We arrived early for the visitation the next night. It was the first time I got to see Frank. I punched him on the shoulder and, through tears, fussed at him. "Why in the world did you not tie yourself onto that tree??? You know better!" I lingered for a bit, talking to him and praying. Then I put the obligatory black comb from his oldest son in his inside pocket (he ALWAYS had one of those combs), kissed his forehead, squeezed his hands, and left the room. That was VERY difficult!

> *For God has not given us a spirit of fear, but of power and of love and of a sound mind.* (2 Timothy 1:7 NKJV)

Two tall chairs were placed at the end of the closed casket, so two of us could sit and still be tall enough to hug and greet our family and friends. I greeted everyone. The chair next to me was empty sometimes and, at other times, filled with one family member or the other. It was an amazing night! Frank was very loved, and so were we.

Some friends from our church in Tampa drove to Atlanta for the funeral, including Jennifer's youth minister.

You know how God is always working, always looking out for you when you don't even realize it?

Read on:

The church administrator came through the visitation line and introduced himself. He asked me if Frank had mentioned a settlement to a small dispute concerning his paychecks.

I answered, "Yes, he told me it was all settled but not how it was settled."

He told me they had decided the church would provide a life insurance policy for Frank that was to go into effect May 1 but would only apply until he turned 70, the following February 22. He repeated that the life insurance policy was to start on May 1. However, a few weeks prior, the effective date had been changed from May 1 to March 1. So, Frank had life insurance from March 1 to March 5, the day he died. And because his death was an accident, it was double indemnity.

WOW! I was speechless! For God to orchestrate all that for us to be taken care of was almost unbelievable!

Joy, Unspeakable!

The funeral was amazing and difficult!

Frank's twin sister Francis, spoke and described being twins in their little hometown of Gastonia, North Carolina. They were quite the rarity. It was very sweet.

Jennifer played his favorite song on the piano—a concert transcription of "Sweet Hour of Prayer." It was not an easy song to play, but one Frank loved, and it brought us all to tears.

We drove an hour to the private family cemetery in Jonesboro, Georgia, where Frank was laid to rest. Many friends from Jonesboro who could not attend the funeral service came to the cemetery. The graveside service was nice, with a Masonic service and the United States flag folded for us since Frank was a veteran. It was not an easy day, to say the least. But we were surrounded by still more family.

Joy Unspeakable in the midst of a tragedy!

. . . .

After Frank's death, we continued to experience God's joy through His protection and provision.

We prepared to sell the house in Atlanta with the help of many friends, but the process still required our frequent travel from Tampa to Atlanta. A couple of weeks after Frank's death, I drove the eight hours to Atlanta in our Tahoe SUV. When I pulled up the hill into our cul-de-sac, I put the front tires on the curb of our driveway and got out to get the mail, leaving the car on and the door open. Suddenly, the car started moving backward! I turned around in a panic, reaching in the door with my hand for the brake as the vehicle was too tall to jump in while moving. I imagined the car going across the cul-de-sac and down the hill into the front door of the house across the way! But the car door went over me as the car kept slowly rolling, finally stopping within just a whisper of the telephone pole.

I got up, shaking like a leaf. My neighbor was on her front porch screaming and trying to call the EMTs, sure that I was dead, "just like Frank 2 weeks ago!" I assured her I was ok, got into the car, and drove up the driveway. I sat there for a few minutes, calming down and getting the courage to look at the back of the car. I got out, petrified to see what I had done. But there was NO damage to the car! None!

Through tears, I looked down at myself and saw that my light tan pants had tire tread marks up the side of my right leg. My hand, which I had held out, was not touched at all. When I got in the house and looked at my bare leg, there were some pretty serious bruises, but no blood, no broken bones, and no car in the doorway of the house across the cul-de-sac! I was blessed beyond words. My arm and hand could have and should have been crushed, not to mention my leg, but I was ok.

Joy Unspeakable in the midst of a tragedy!

. . . .

As we continued to prepare the house to sell, we had a room left that needed to be painted. We knew a painter in Tampa that a friend had used many times. His name was Dean, and he did a good job, and was honest. I explained to my friend I could not have him stay at my house in Atlanta because that would not be proper. I just needed to find a Dean in Atlanta.

So, Jennifer and I begrudgingly decided that it was up to us to finish the job. We flew to Atlanta and took the rapid transit train from the airport to the train station close to our house, where a friend was poised to pick us up and take us home.

We got on the train at the airport terminal and were glad only four people were in our car, giving us room for our bags. At the first stop, the door opened, and another passenger got on—a younger man wearing painting overalls with a lot of paint on them. He could have sat anywhere, but he sat down on the seat next to me. Trying to be polite, I said, "I am going to look like that tomorrow."

He said, "Oh, you are painting tomorrow?"

I said, "Yes, we are painting our den."

Then he said, "I will paint it for you for $40." He had not even asked the size of the room or anything at this point. "Do you have brushes, paint, and a ladder?"

I replied, "Yes."

"Can I get there on the rapid transit train?"

I said, "Yes, close enough for us to pick you up."

He said, "Ok, I will paint it for you tomorrow." Then he looked at the train schedule and said, "I can be there at 8:30 am. Can you pick me up then?"

I answered, "Yes."

He said, "Ok."

Jennifer and I were amazed and shocked.

He said, "Just so you know I am not kidding and so you know you don't have anything to worry about, here's my driver's license." When I took it out of his hand and looked at the name... His name was Dean!

Jennifer and I were shocked! God sent us a Dean in Atlanta to do our painting after all!

We picked him up the next morning, stopped to get coffee, and we accomplished our task in much less time than we could have done. Dean was very nice. We ministered to him rather than him ministering to us! And he did not just paint one wall, we also painted a bigger room in the house that was severely in need of painting. We spent the entire day painting with him and thanking God for sending us provision when we needed it.

. . . .

So, were we devastated that Frank was gone? ABSOLUTELY!

Of course, there were times of sadness, but we had many more times of wonderful memories!

I would cry in the shower, asking God how I was going to provide for Jennifer alone. The enemy did everything he could to keep me from succeeding in taking care of us. I didn't want to go anywhere for a while except work and church. It was a chore even to go grocery shopping, so Jennifer did most of that for us.

But God continued to show us He was in charge. He put people in place to do things that I would not have known how to do or that I could not do. He kept us involved in our church and allowed us to go forward with joy because we could see His hand at work then and now! He never stops taking care of His children!

> *For I am persuaded that neither death nor life, nor angels nor principalities nor powers, nor things to present nor things to come, nor height nor depth, nor any other created thing, shall be able to separate us from the love of God which is in Christ Jesus our Lord.* (Romans 8:38-39 NKJV)

Now, for the rest of the story:

God found us a beautiful home in Tampa that was just perfect for us. It had a pool and was close to our church, so our friends from church could stop by often. And, He found a buyer for the house in Atlanta. Jennifer got a full scholarship to attend a local university and found her passion in computer engineering. In 2008 I married my Sunday School teacher whose wife had died unexpectedly shortly after Frank. I acquired two more daughters. The oldest is single and lives with her mother in Texas. The other two live close to us. Our middle daughter has three children, ages 15, 14, and 10.

And Jennifer? Well, Jennifer married the cute guitar player in our youth praise band at church after dating for a while. He is now the music minister and youth minister at our church. They have two daughters, ages 3 and 5.

The enemy was ABSOLUTELY at work.

But when you recognize God's hand at work and know that the Creator of the universe is on your side and in your heart, the enemy does not have a chance.

I remember the 23rd Psalm from learning it at a very early age. It has always been a big part of my strength.

Psalm 23:1-6 NKJV

> *The LORD is my shepherd; I shall not want. He makes me to lie down in green pastures; He leads me beside the still waters. He restores my soul; He leads me in the paths of righteousness For His name's sake. Yea, though I walk through the valley of the shadow of death, I will fear no evil; for You are with me; Your rod and Your staff, they comfort me. You prepare a table before me in the presence of my enemies; You anoint my head with oil; My cup runs over. Surely goodness and mercy shall follow me all the days of my life; and I will dwell in the house of the LORD forever.* (Romans 8:38-39 NKJV)

Sometimes in this life, we will walk through tragedy, but the Lord is always with us. And when we cling to Him, we *will* find joy.

Joy in His Comfort

As we walk through life's daily trials, we need to know how to find comfort in God and understand that He can comfort us in the chaos. Despite the many situations we all walk through—suffering, sorrow, or grief—our most loving God is always our source of comfort. We can hold on to the pillow of security He provides because, as His children, we are sealed in His casing.

How is it that God is our ever-source of comfort? He is because He gave us His Son, Jesus Christ, as the sacrifice and payment for our sins.

> *But Christ proved God's passionate love for us by dying in our place while we were still lost and ungodly!* (Romans 5:8 TPT)

Perhaps we can be more receptive to experiencing joy in His comfort when we recognize that the God who sent Christ for us while we were sinners is the same God who still watches over us! God already gave us His Son, and our joy associated with this is powerful, a stronghold we can cling to because God is always with us. God sent us the Holy Spirit when we confessed with our mouths, trusted, and believed in Him. At that very moment, He became our Comforter.

When we need a quick solution to the chaos in our life, we can shift our focus by going right to God's Word, which reframes our perspective by reminding us of who God is and what He did for each of us personally. Even though suffering is a part of life because we live in a world of sin, our story does not have to end there.

> *For as we share abundantly in Christ's sufferings, so through Christ we share abundantly in comfort too.* (2 Corinthians 1:5 ESV)

When Jesus redeems us, we become part of His victorious story. We share in the joy of being comforted by Him, knowing that our sufferings and sorrow will be replaced with endless joy when we go home to be with Jesus.

If you are hurting at this very moment and in need of the comfort of your Heavenly Father, remember He loves you. Let's pray this prayer together. Pray it for yourself or for someone else God is putting on your heart:

Dear Lord Jesus,

You are the God of comfort. You are solid, unchanging in Your nature and character, forever holding to Your promises. I need an anchor to help me through my suffering and sorrow—You are my anchor. Bring me support and comfort, and steady me with Your presence. Show me through Your Word a scripture that will get me through this tough time. Even when I don't understand why I am struggling, I know that You, God, are in control, and Your sovereign will is happening. I know that through the Holy Spirit, I am sealed; I am your child for all eternity because Jesus died for my sins, and I have been forgiven through repentance. I choose now to live for You. I know You will comfort me in my time of need because I am asking You to. Your Word is full of promises. I believe them to be true for my life. Please pour out over me Your joy of comfort through the power of Your Word, alive in scripture. I trust You as my ultimate source of joy to comfort me through every storm.

In Jesus' name, I pray. Amen.

The mighty Spirit of the Lord Yahweh is wrapped around me because Yahweh has anointed me, as a messenger to preach good news to the poor.

He sent me to heal the wounds of the brokenhearted, to tell captives, "You are free," and to tell prisoners, "Be free from your darkness."

I am sent to announce a new season of Yahweh's grace and a time of God's recompense on his enemies, to comfort all who are in sorrow, to strengthen those crushed by despair who mourn in Zion—to give them a beautiful bouquet in the place of ashes, the oil of bliss instead of tears, and the mantle of joyous praise instead of the spirit of happiness.

Because of this, they will be known as Mighty Oaks of Righteousness, planted by Yahweh as a living display of His glory. (Isaiah 61:1-3 TPT)

Janet Harllee

Janet Harllee is a storyteller, broadcaster, speaker, and author. She has a passion to share God's truth delivering to her audiences encouraging, inspirational and entertaining messages of faith in an ever-changing world. Sometimes these messages are through Janet's character, Mitsy Lou Puppernickel, a Southern hairdresser. Her other experiences include theatre, radio, and television.

Janet is currently the host of her broadcast, "Faith in An Ever-Changing World- encouragement & hope", where she interviews people who share what God has given them to do in this season and how faith is helping them do it.

Janet is also a member of Women World Leaders, a unified global women's ministry empowering one another to follow Christ, to love in abundance, and to cultivate women warriors in purpose, His promises, and His power.

She enjoys exercising, having coffee breaks with friends, making new friends, and using her God-given talents to create projects to glorify Him.

You can connect with Janet on these social media outlets:

Faith In An Ever-Changing World-encouragement & hope | Facebook

Janet Harllee - YouTube

Joy in Aging

by Janet Harllee

Working in retirement communities for 20 years, I have been blessed to learn from the exuberance and zest of the residents that our age is not a barrier to the life of joy that God calls us to lead.

Maybe my most impactful lesson came from a lady in her 90s who had a remarkably positive attitude about where she was in her life. This tiny stature of a woman had age-related macular degeneration. According to the American Academy of Ophthalmology, this condition occurs when part of the retina, called the macula, is damaged, causing a loss of central vision and, eventually, eyesight. But this lady learned her way around her room, how to get to the dining room, beauty shop, and other areas. She met each day thanking God and did not let losing her sight stop her from participating in activities and living in joy, knowing her time was short. David said in the book of Psalms, *Indeed, You have made my days as handbreadths, And my age is as nothing before You; Certainly every man at his best state is but vapor. Selah* (Psalm 39:5 NKJV)

My mother, who had Alzheimer's, lived in our memory care center for three years - until she was 98. Mother was a godly woman whose devastating disease had far-reaching effects in our family. Still, it was evident that God gave her joy in those last years through the friendships He provided in her home away from home.

One year, the community had five residents who were 100 years old. One of those residents, who didn't look to be 100, was a veteran, a kind gentleman who read his Bible every day. The question of why he was still here walking this earth was always on his mind. But that man was always talking to other residents about God. It was clear God was still with him and using him for His purpose—reminding me that God has a purpose for every day of our lives. *Even when I am old and gray, do not forsake me, my God, till I declare your power to the next generation, your mighty acts to all who are to come. Your righteousness, God, reaches to the heavens, you who have done great things. Who is like you, God?* (Psalm 71:18-19 NIV)

Joy comes, for the residents, in the little things. There is a day school on campus, and children from the school visit the residents daily, lighting up their faces with smiles. The activity director provides opportunities for outings—to Candor in the Sandhills of North Carolina, to purchase fresh peaches, to visit the NC State Zoo, or to go to the Southern Supreme Fruitcake Factory in Bear Creek, NC. The residents have ridden in the Veterans Day and Christmas parades, gleefully waving at everyone along the route. During the holidays, the activity director takes them to see the wonder of Christmas lights in surrounding neighborhoods. The chaplain holds a Fall and Spring revival for the residents. And the activity room is packed each night. I can remember one gentleman, who was in his 80s, accepting Jesus as his Savior at one of these services. That just goes to prove that it is never too late to come to Christ. At times I had the joy and opportunity to go to a resident's room and just sit and listen to them. It made their day. And it always brightened mine.

Additionally, the community has a project called *Dream Makers*. The mission is to, as much as possible, make their residents' dreams come true. For example, a man in his late 60s and a woman in her early or mid-90s wanted to skydive. So they did! And then they wanted to do it again. Both of them could not stop talking about their dream that had come true. Then a lady in her mid-80s got to see her sister for her birthday celebration—for the first time in 40 years. What a joyful reunion. Other realized dreams included a few men who went to Atlanta Braves baseball games and a married couple in their early 90s who had lunch where they spent their honeymoon. It gives me joy just remembering and sharing with you these wonderful times.

I learned so much from my years working with seniors. Here are just a few things.

1. Never lose faith in God

Seniors have lived a lot of life, filled with both the good and the bad. They have stories to share. When we take the time to listen, we show them they are valued, and we gain wisdom from their experiences. Stories I've heard—such as those from the Great Depression, surviving after the death of a child, and finding joy in the day-to-day—have taught me how faith and trust in God can carry us through. Like this scripture says, *Rejoice always, pray constantly, give thanks in everything; for this is God's will for you in Christ Jesus.* (1 Thessalonians 5:16-18 CSB)

2. You have value

Some seniors feel that when they get older, they lose their value—feeling they no longer have a purpose. We need to encourage others and ourselves daily, knowing God values each of us always, and when we don't appreciate that, we miss out. *Do not cast me off in the time of old age; Do not forsake me when my strength fails.* (Psalm 71:9 NKJV)

3. Slow your steps

I always walk fast, just like my mother. When I walked past a senior in my hurried way, they always told me to slow my steps. Seeing the residents with walkers or in wheelchairs, I could envision myself, recognizing that my day will come when my steps will be at a slower pace. But maybe it's okay to slow down today—to walk peacefully through each day, aware of the wonders of God all around us.

4. Relationships matter
Some families I worked with were broken, leaving the residents with no one to advocate for them. Others had sons or daughters who had not spoken to or seen them in several years. Then other families were always visiting and loving on their loved ones. But God made us for community, and relationships require work, forgiveness, and persistence. Don't give up on people—we weren't meant to do life alone.

5. Joy is in the little things
A smile. A hug. Someone spending time with us. As we go through life, we need to take good care of ourselves and pay attention to the little things. Ladies who kept their weekly hair appointments and continued their routine of putting make-up on every day seemed to feel better about themselves. They stayed young at heart. God wants us to find joy in the everyday. Jesus said, *"I have told you these things so that my joy may be in you and your joy may be complete."* (John 15:11 CSB)

6. Serve God where you are
As we each grow older, we always have the opportunity to serve God right where we are. Look around and see where God is calling you. One of the most significant ways we are called to serve is to be strong prayer warriors. Whatever your walk of life, God has called you to pray for your community, country, world, and the so many people who are sick and in need. Prayer brings results that make a huge difference.

Some time back, I remember reading a magazine article about aging. It showed pictures of women's shapes at different ages. I told myself that I would never look like that! Then one day, I stepped out of the shower and caught a glimpse of myself in the mirror. Page 24 flashed before my eyes. I'll be honest with you—I do not like the changes that aging is bringing.

You have heard the saying, "getting older is not for wimps." It's true. I know. I point to the scripture, which states, *Charm is deceptive, and beauty is fleeting; but a woman who fears the LORD is to be praised.* (Proverbs 31:30 NIV) Every morning when I look in the mirror, I see another wrinkle. I feel my body changing. After a sleepless night, I don't function as well. Dark spots, called age spots, appear on my face, legs, and arms overnight. There are things I cannot do like I used to. Sometimes I walk deliberately into a room and then forget why I went there. Where is the joy in all of this?

It is a fact that we are all getting older. Aging is just one of life's transitions or seasons. Since there is no way to avoid aging, I have decided to embrace it and rely on God's promise, *I will be the same until your old age, and I will bear you up when you turn gray. I have made you, and I will carry you; I will bear and rescue you.* (Isaiah 46:4 CSB) These words from our Lord stay close to my heart.

I asked some of my friends who are aging along with me about their joy in aging.

Bobbie says, "How do you empower yourself to keep your body healthy and prepared to always do God's work? As we journey down the path of aging, we will face obstacles. Those obstacles can define us if we let them. I have chosen joy to define me over obstacles. Yes, I am still aging, but I am surrounding myself with joy in the process. No matter how our day goes, we all have one thing in common. We get out of bed. We each have our own way to start the day God has blessed us with. My joy grows each morning as I walk at daybreak—two and a half miles, eight laps around our pond. Each lap embraces a different person or situation in prayer. Because of several health issues, I had to stop walking for a while, but I measured my recovery on when I could work my way back up to the eight laps. I could have stopped walking, but my joy as I spend time with the Lord in the morning as I age is a blessing I hope to never want to give up."

Renea says, "What brings me joy is that God has allowed me to travel, speak, and share His love and laughter all over the world." Her main scripture is, *A joyful heart is good medicine, but a broken spirit dries up the bones.* (Proverbs 17:22 CSB) Renea's joy is also time spent with her grandchildren and listening to the interesting and fun facts they share about life.

Sylvia says, "Two of my greatest joys are my husband—the love of my life, and the outdoors! I love taking photos of God's beauty in simple things, such as a flower, a butterfly, a hummingbird, or small insects. I have chased butterflies for years with a camera in hand, and I continue to research and identify numerous butterflies, insects, and flowers to learn about them. My love of books never ceases." Sylvia continues, "Additional joy comes from helping promote the art of storytelling. I enjoy keeping my mind active."

While shopping at a favorite thrift store, I went by the manager's office, who is a good friend of mine and a senior. She told me that she and her husband are having some challenging times due to her husband's severe car accident. His physical and mental abilities were affected. It is one day at a time. God's Word tells us to, *Consider it a great joy, my brothers and sisters, whenever you experience various trials, because you know that the testing of your faith produces endurance. And let endurance have its full effect, so that you may be mature and complete, lacking nothing.* (James 1:2-4 CSB) She said she could not go through this without the Lord. As I was leaving her office, I saw a sign on the wall that said, 'Choose Joy.' We both laughed.

God's work is never done. When I retired, I asked the Lord, "What do you want me to do next?" He laid a broadcast on my heart, "Faith In An Ever-Changing World - Encouragement & Hope." I felt led to talk to people about their faith stories. It could be how faith got them through a situation or their testimony. Stories are important, and they are universal.

One guest shared she was kidnapped at a young age and was found several years later. When she found Jesus, she found forgiveness. Another guest told of retiring from a job with great benefits and salary to step out on faith into an evangelistic ministry. A couple gave their testimony of getting married, getting divorced, and how God brought them together again a few years later—now they minister to other couples. Men and women have shared how faith in God gave them the strength to never give up. Still other stories have been about life experiences, such as losing a child, being abused, and living a life of drugs, partying, and sin. There are so many more stories and future stories to come. When we tell our story, we tell His. One thing all my guests' stories have in common is that salvation changed their life and allowed living to begin. Doing this broadcast is a joy and a blessing. It allows me to meet and get to know so many brothers and sisters in Christ. Paul said to the people in the church at Corinth, *Therefore, my dear brothers and sisters, be steadfast, immovable, always excelling in the Lord's work, because you know that your labor in the Lord is not in vain.* (1 Corinthians 15:58 CSB) I want to continue being faithful to do it until God gives me another assignment.

Life is short no matter what age you are. Life keeps on going, and all of a sudden, here I am in the fourth quarter of my life. How did I get here so fast? What used to be important is not as important now. It is not a big house, a good-paying job, getting ahead, collecting stuff, or receiving awards that create joy in my life. So, where do I find joy in aging? Now, the joy in my life is rising to meet another day God has given, meeting friends for coffee, taking care of my plants and flowers, and feeding the birds. My joy is my family and friends, serving my church, exercising, and working on creative projects God continues to give me. I know I can be joyful in all situations because Christ lives in me. He is my true joy. He loves me, wrinkles and all. And, right now, He has blessed me with good health. I ask Him to use me up, and with all the talents and skills He has given me, to bring glory to Him and His kingdom.

Aging is not easy. There are no magic creams to get rid of wrinkles. Your appearance and body will continue to change. Like the scriptures say, *So we do not lose heart. Though our outer self is wasting away, our inner self is being renewed day by day.* (2 Corinthians 4:16 ESV) I admit that I am still learning to accept these changes and be confident in who I am and what is happening as I try to grow older gracefully. I love what the book of Psalms tells us, *Teach us to number our days, that we may gain a heart of wisdom.* (Psalm 90:12 NIV)

Just because I am not working anymore at a professional business or organization does not mean I have to sit in a rocking chair and give up. I have learned there is value in growing older. God has prepared me for such a time as this. He is still using me for His purpose. He has said, *They will still bear fruit in old age, healthy and green.* (Psalm 92:14 CSB) I am looking forward to my latter days being greater. He tells us in His Word, *Then, even if your beginnings were modest, your final days will be full of prosperity.* (Job 8:7 CSB) If you are in your latter years, be encouraged. Joy is in a lifelong fellowship with God. *You reveal the path of life to me; in your presence is abundant joy; at your right hand are eternal pleasures.* (Psalm 16:11 (CSB)

When my work is done here, my complete joy will be eternal life with Jesus, *For God so loved the world that He gave His one and only Son, that whoever believes in Him shall not perish but have eternal life.* (John 3:16 NIV) In the meantime, I will continue to run the race toward the prize and be able to say, *I have fought the good fight, I have finished the race, I have kept the faith.* (2 Timothy 4:7 NIV)

Recently, I heard a story on a Christian radio station about a man in his 90s who had moved into a retirement community. He had been a musician in his professional life and still actively played. So, he searched out other residents who were musicians or who could play an instrument and formed a band. Their band plays for both their community and outside the community, bringing laughter and joy wherever they are. The radio hosts talked about joy, commenting that joy is all around us. Sometimes we just have to look for it.

On my refrigerator door, there is a magnetic sign that reminds me every day to "Choose Joy."

I choose joy. What about you?

Joy in Our Victories

The word victory is a happy one. It is defined as overcoming, winning in a competition or a struggle, or rising above difficult problems. The Bible teaches us that we have already been given the victory in Christ Jesus.

> *For everyone born of God overcomes the world. This is the victory that has overcome the world, even our faith.* (1 John 5:4 NIV)

Victories in our lives come because God is with us. His presence as Lord in our life is all we need to succeed. Examples in the Word, such as King David, show God's preservation of His people. King David stayed faithful to God, and he was victorious because the Lord blessed him, protected him, and prospered him.

> *But let all those rejoice who put their trust in You; Let them ever shout for joy, because You defend them; Let those also who love Your name be joyful in You. For You, O LORD, will bless the righteous; With favor You will surround him as with a shield.* (Psalm 5:11-12 NKJV)

Finding joy from a place of victory in our lives is not something we fight for—it is something we receive by faith. God does the work for us, in us, and through us by the Holy Spirit. According to God, victory is already yours in

Jesus Christ! By having faith in Jesus Christ and His work on the cross, you and I have victory over sin, darkness, and death. Victory does not come to us through our own works, special commitments, or sacrifices. Jesus is our power to overcome sin and be victorious. When we allow Jesus to live through us, we can be joyful, knowing the victory is ours. Jesus does not just "give" us victory; the Bible is noticeably clear, Jesus IS our victory.

> *Yet in all these things we are more than conquerors through Him who loved us.* (Romans 8:37 NKJV)

> *But thanks be to God, who gives us the victory through our Lord Jesus Christ.* (1 Corinthians 15:57 NKJV)

Please do not spend your life thinking you will get the victory by fighting for it and wrestling with the devil at every confrontation he sizes you up in. You will end up miserable and at a devastating loss. Joy in victories is ours through faith.

Just like King David, your victory will come because God is with you. My victories only come because God is with me. I have nothing to be afraid of. My battles have already been won by Christ's death on the cross—the payment for my sin. I can have joy in every victory I receive, recognizing that each one is from God. All the joy you and I experience in our victories is because we know, beyond a doubt, that God abides in us, and it is He who has overcome the world.

. . . .

Nette

Nette is a mother of three and a registered nurse from New England who presently lives in Florida.

Nette is passionate about sharing how her life challenges brought her closer to God and how God can use any situation for His glory. She enjoys reading, the outdoors, music, spending alone time with God, and serving others.

Joy in the Midst of Loneliness

by Nette

For many, loneliness comes like a thief in the night—sudden and uninvited. For others, it can slowly creep into our lives, creating its own long, drawn-out season. Loneliness attempts to steal our joy and rob our peace—without regard to how it arrived. But by being willing to grow through our emotions, we can turn the tables. By changing our perspective and abiding in Christ, loneliness can strengthen our relationship with God and birth a purpose of impacting others for Jesus Christ.

In life, it is not unusual to feel forgotten, betrayed, scorned, unappreciated, or even unloved. These circumstances can leave us in a deep pit that is difficult to dig out of. As a result, we may experience a loss of "happiness." I used to confuse happiness with joy, living in bondage through repeated cycles of loneliness. But then a change happened. God drew me closer to Him, transformed me, and taught me how to receive the joy of the Lord. I began looking to Him to fill the emptiness inside and stopped trying to fill it with people, careers, or things. I learned there is no substitute for God as He embraced me and let me experience *in Your presence is fullness of joy*. (Psalm 16:11 NKJV) God will often allow what is necessary to bring us back to where we ought to be in Him.

I have experienced many seasons of loneliness, from a carefree young child to a busy and burnt-out middle-aged adult, but for a long time, I refused to pay attention to what God was trying to teach me. Loneliness impacted me differently in middle age, causing me to search deep inside to get answers to those tough questions. What was I running from? Why was I feeling alone? What unresolved issues needed to be addressed? It was not easy to uncover these answers, but it was necessary to do the work. The process would be well worth it.

My first experience with loneliness came when I had to play by myself as a young child. Often I sat by myself in an apartment, shifting from one single-parent home to the other. One parent worked two jobs, and the other was emotionally unavailable due to the psychological effects of severe trauma. Then, I experienced loneliness as a young adult after moving into my first apartment, and later again in a failed marriage that started wrong and ended even worse. Loneliness showed up in mid-life when I became estranged from the ones I loved most and burnt out from a career that constantly drained my energy, leaving little time for anything else. It seemed as if "lonely" would never leave me alone.

In my childhood, I was well provided for—a clean home, plenty of food to eat, clothing to wear, and lots of toys and "things" to keep me occupied. However, I lacked the expression of love and affection through intimate relationships with those who were very important to me—my parents and siblings. I often felt alone in this huge world, and I had an empty hole on the inside. My parents were hardworking but not big on hugs, kisses, or words of affirmation. I don't remember ever hearing "I love you." I have since learned that love, affection, and affirmation are essential to raising children, but at the time, my life seemed normal. I coped by staying in the largest room of the house, falling asleep with the TV or radio on as I held my baby doll tightly and sucked on two fingers for comfort. On the nights I couldn't sleep, I would listen to music or clean the house as best I could. I also made cards, drew pictures, and created dance routines for my parents. I see now that those were all attempts to please my parents—in hopes of receiving their love, affection, and affirmation and gaining some quality time to help me escape loneliness.

I had an older sibling who I looked up to. I followed her wherever she and her crew went, traveling just far enough behind to not be noticed. Eventually, I would get discovered and sent back home to be alone again. Despite wanting my sibling to include me, our relationship was ruined early on.

The ones I loved most either shunned me or did not know how to show their love in ways that were nurturing. It seemed I did not matter to anyone. I felt like I was in a dark, cold, lonely room with no way to escape. These experiences impacted my future behavior, as I vacillated between navigating never being alone and avoidance of others. The bottom line is that I feared being hurt by others. As a young child, I wrote letters to God for comfort and dropped them in the mailbox in front of our house addressed "Heaven." I don't recall what I wrote in those letters, but I believed God would read them and answer me.

As a young adult, I resisted moving out of my parent's home. I stayed as long as I could—until about the age of twenty-five. I feared living alone. When I did move out, I did not adjust well and never stayed home. To the world, I was "successful." I had finished my secondary education and was doing well in my career, but I still lacked the intimate relationships God created us to have. I worked a lot and went out as much as I could, only to be home long enough to rest, cook, eat, and then go back out again. I sought the presence of others constantly to bring me joy.

My early relationships never lasted long, as no person could ever fulfill my constant need for love and affection. Later, when I got married, I thought my loneliness would be cured. Surely my new family—mother, father, and siblings-in-law—would send my loneliness packing for good. Unfortunately, this was not the case, for I was shunned, disregarded, and treated like an outsider. I recall sitting alone at family gatherings and church. To my dismay, it was clear I was not of their culture and did not fit into their box. Once again, I found myself feeling alone. Yet another relationship I cared deeply about lacked intimacy. Yes, you can feel loneliness in marriage, too. It was clear that we both got married for the wrong reasons. But I remained in the marriage for too long, fearing the effects on my children. I did not want them to grow up with their parents in separate households, feeling alone and unloved. I learned there is no room for fear when we walk in God's will, and as parents, we can entrust our children to Him.

After my marriage ended, I had to care for my three children as a single parent while I juggled work and cared for an elderly parent. My numerous responsibilities kept me so occupied that I was too busy to notice the loneliness hidden and tucked away deep inside. It was only in those late-night quiet moments, when everyone was asleep, that loneliness would peek its head out and say, "Hey, I'm still here."

As my children grew older and my parents went on to be with the Lord, my loneliness became more apparent. Now a middle-aged woman, I had fewer responsibilities and more free time, leaving me feeling empty with no sense of peace or happiness. I tried to reconnect with old friends to no avail, as most had moved or experienced changes in their life circumstances. I found myself deep in a pit of loneliness, lacking intimate relationships and longing for the emptiness to be filled.

> *"The thief comes only to steal and kill and destroy; I have come that they may have life, and have it to the full."* (John 10:10 NIV)

Mr. Thief knew where I lived and even had the key to get in. Loneliness moved into the spare bedroom and came out now and then, feeding off my despair in isolation. I had felt very alone as a child, in my young adulthood, and in my marriage. In mid-life, it was difficult for others to get close to me due to my fears, which further deepened the pit within me. I lacked the intimate relationships that God created us to have. I eventually became isolated, only maximizing my loneliness and weariness. Joy was nowhere to be found, for I had chosen to travel the path of wallowing in my circumstances instead of looking beyond and looking to God. Like the psalmist wrote in Psalm 88:14-18, I felt rejected and weary.

In all these different stages in my life, loneliness stole my joy as I ran in fear, trying to replace it with people, responsibilities, work, and things. I came to the point of great despair. Having lost hope that my situation would ever change, I was ready to give up. I wanted my breath to literally stop.

Then I got a nudge in my spirit to attend an inner-city church. I obeyed, and when I found out there was a women's conference the following week, I went. At the conference, the speaker spoke the words, "I don't know who this is for, but I came all this way to tell you that God does not want you to hold your breath... don't give up... He is working in you and will restore you." The tears rolled down my face as I was reminded that God saw me and knew what I had been going through. I was not alone.

After leaving the conference, I began recognizing and becoming receptive to God's voice teaching and comforting me. His Word says in Isaiah 42:5 and Acts 17:25 that *Jesus is the breath of life*. Through this breath, I stopped placing my hope in the perishable—relationships, work, and material things—and began putting my hope in the imperishable things of God—my intimate, spiritual relationship with Him.

I learned to depend on God's Word, and Matthew 6:33 says, *But seek ye first the kingdom of God, and His righteousness; and all these things shall be added unto you.* (KJV) In my studies, I found out that one of these things Christians receive is JOY. I cried out to God with rivers of tears pouring down my cheeks, screaming, "Enough is enough." I humbled myself before God and pleaded for His help. I still, to this day, continue to cry out and seek God.

One day, I unmistakably heard a soft whisper and felt His embrace. I knew He heard my cry and that He had kept those letters I wrote to Him as a child, waiting for me to be receptive to His response. God prompted me to do some self-reflection. Could it be that He had to remove those things in my life that took His place? Those things brought only temporary happiness, but God wanted to give me everlasting joy. He was certainly trying to get my attention, but for what purpose? He revealed that He could use my loneliness purposefully, drawing me to seek Him. In the letters I wrote as a child, a seed was planted. Then, later, on my knees with tears, those seeds began to grow.

God also taught me that I only experience His presence of joy when I abide in Him. You see, even though I had accepted Jesus Christ as my Lord and Savior as a teenager, I was not always living a life in Christ. God is a righteous God, and sin separates us from Him. When we do not abide in Him—when we don't seek, trust, or obey His commands—we become distant from Him, resulting in loneliness.

> *"Abide in Me... If you abide in Me, and My words abide in you, you will ask what you desire, and it shall be done for you."* (John 15:4, 7 NKJV)

We can abide in God by spending time with Him daily in prayer, worship, and studying the Word. How do you begin your day? Prioritizing God ensures there will be no idols in your life replacing Him, whether it's a career, spouse, children, personal goals, or even ministry. The first verse written down in my first Bible gifted to me was Matthew 6:33, *But seek ye first the kingdom of God, and His righteousness; and all these things shall be added unto you.* (KJV) When we are careful to put God first, everything else will fall into place. Perhaps your state of loneliness is because you expected other things—"idols"—to fill the empty space. We are to seek God first!

I've learned to abide by remaining focused on the right things. Forget the former things; *do not dwell on the past. See, I am doing a new thing! Now it springs up; do you not perceive it?* (Isaiah 43:18-19 NIV) Sometimes in our loneliness, we lose joy because our thoughts remain in the past instead of hoping in the present and future of God's promises. I often prolonged the process and intensified the pain of loneliness as a result of those very actions. *Delight yourself in the LORD, and He will give you the desires of your heart.* (Psalm 37:4 ESV)

Lastly, loneliness can result from having the wrong mindset or perspective. I often gave more thought to the situation instead of seeking the purpose. I grew weary as my vision became blurry and I could not understand what I was going through. I began to lose hope as I lost sight.

Paul wrote in 2 Timothy 4:16 *At my first defense, no one came to my support, but everyone deserted me. May it not be held against them.* (NIV) Paul, too, felt abandoned and alone; however, he maintained the right perspective as he recognized that God was with him, strengthening him to fulfill his purpose of sharing the gospel of Jesus Christ. Had Paul not had the proper perspective, many people would not have been reached with the gospel.

It is important to look through a spiritual lens at our seasons of loneliness. Often, we can't understand how God is using our times of suffering; this is where trust and faith in God come in as a part of abiding in Him. We must trust and have faith that everything will work towards our good, as it says in Romans 8:28, *And we know that all things work together for good to those who love God, to those who are called according to His purpose.* (NKJV)

Remaining faithful will also help us retain a hopeful perspective. *In Him our hearts rejoice, for we trust in His holy name.* (Psalm 33:21 NIV) *Set your mind on things above, not on things on the earth.* (Colossians 3:2 NKJV) Having the proper perspective during seasons of loneliness will allow God's purpose to be fulfilled in our lives.

Through God's grace, I no longer cry tears of pain from loneliness but tears of joy, regardless of loneliness. Like the caterpillar is transformed into a marvelous butterfly while alone in its cocoon, I recognize that I, too, am being transformed by my Creator, set aside by Him to complete a marvelous work.

If you are feeling lonely, know that you are never alone. There is no place in the universe where God cannot find us, no pit deep enough that He cannot pull us out. Where can I go from your Spirit? *Where can I flee from your presence? If I go up to the heavens, you are there; if I make my bed in the depths, you are there. If I rise on the wings of the dawn, if I settle on the far side of the sea, even there your hand will guide me, your right hand will hold me fast.* (Psalm 139:7-10 NIV)

We need only to open our hearts to let Him in. God's Word is full of writings to encourage us. 1 John 1:4 says, *We are writing these things so that our joy may be complete.* (CSB) It brings a person joy to share testimonies of how our struggles transformed into blessings. When we speak of God's transforming work in us, that power gives freedom of joy as we offer up praise and thanksgiving instead of complaints and resistance. Let us be willing to encourage ourselves amid loneliness by receiving the joy that comes from focusing on the Creator, not the creation.

Do you have a story of God overcoming loneliness in your life? If so, are you willing to share with others about your challenging season? How might God use your experience to impact others? I hope this chapter has encouraged you to write your own story to impact another.

When we abide in Him and keep the right perspective as we grow through our stage of loneliness, we can experience the joy that comes only from God. When we recognize that our joy is rooted only in our relationship with God, He will allow our lives to be transformed into purpose. We must not resist the process or waddle in the pain, but we must trust the Creator.

What is God wanting to transform in you?

Heavenly Father, may You help us discover that we are never alone when we abide in You. Help us not to resist the process of this season, and help us to trust You in it. May we also recognize that our loneliness has a purpose so we can have the right perspective. Then we will be able to join with the psalmist, singing, *The Lord has done great things for us, and we are filled with joy.* (Psalm 126:3 NIV)

Joy in His Love

God's love is steadfast and unchanging. Of course, we can grow distant from Him, changing our ways and attitudes toward Him. But the beauty of God is how much He loves us despite us and our ways. The Bible tells us God loved us while we were still sinners; His love abounds from His infinite goodness and mercy.

Life can be filled with failed relationships, friendships that drift away, and painful separation from family members—all because our love for one another as human beings is ever-changing. But God's love is never changing. Human love can be fickle. We want to feel loved and to experience emotional satisfaction in our love, so we tend to love conditionally and reserve parts of ourselves. When we do this, we inevitably create conditions in which we almost guarantee rejection and pain. And depending on the one we love, we may experience no reciprocation or returned love. Sometimes the love we end up with is superficial, and it is challenging to find any comfort or joy in that kind of love.

The word love is used so much these days, and by extension, it is often cheapened. However, God's love for you is real; it is priceless. His love is sacrificial. So much that He gave His Son in love so that we can live. The infinite God, incarnate as Jesus, loves you infinitely. His love is deep, perfect, steadfast, and unchanging. In God's perfect love, we can find complete *Joy Unspeakable*.

And in that joy, we can have strength as we face the challenges of this world and hold fast to our hope for eternity.

The love of God is far greater than anything we can humanly imagine. God does not just love us when we are good; He loves us unconditionally! Why would He do that when we sin against Him and continually mess up? God loves us because God IS love! His love can not be gained by anything we do. He has always loved you, and He always will love you.

> *But God proves His love for us in this: while we were still sinners, Christ died for us.* (Romans 5:8 CSB)

God's love is immeasurable, bringing us joy in His love. His life, His death for your sins, and His resurrection overcoming death were all so that you might also overcome death. God loves us so much He meets us at our greatest need, even though we are the least worthy of such love. God's love, demonstrated to you on the cross, is just the beginning of having a loving companion for life. No matter what you may go through, He is there. His love is never-changing and ever-available to you.

> *Can anything ever separate us from Christ's love? Does it mean he no longer loves us if we have trouble or calamity, or are persecuted, or hungry, or destitute, or in danger, or threatened with death?* (Romans 8:35 NLT)

Nothing can separate us from the love of God.

> *I am convinced that nothing can ever separate us from God's love. Neither death nor life, neither angels nor demons, neither our fears for today nor our worries about tomorrow—not even the powers of hell can separate us from God's love. No power in the sky above or in the earth below—indeed, nothing in all creation will ever be able to separate us from the love of God that is revealed in Christ Jesus our Lord.* (Romans 8:38-39 NLT)

God wants to bless us with complete joy in His love, but we will never experience the fullness of His love until we give Him the position He deserves in our lives. His love is always with us, but to encounter it, we must humble ourselves in complete surrender to live our lives as He intended, never separated from Him or His love. When you accept God's unconditional love, He will see to it that you are engulfed in true joy!

. . . .

Ann Hall

Ann Hall lives in rural Missouri with her husband of thirty-plus years, Andrew. She has two grown children and one grandson. After a career as a first responder in Florida, where she met her husband who worked as a volunteer fireman and as an emergency room nurse, they decided to move to the countryside for a slower pace of life.

Ann now works as an administrative assistant at her church, where prayer is abundant and faith is a daily conversation. During her time off from work, Ann can be found in the garden with her chickens, cats, and Stella, her Great Pyrenees dog. Stella keeps the coyotes away from the chickens and the deer away from the garden.

Ann and Andrew enjoy cooking together and have perfected a quiche made with their farm-fresh eggs. In the winter, they can be found sledding in the snow with Stella, who helps pull the sled. They feel blessed to be able to enjoy the country lifestyle together.

Why Bother to Pray?

by Ann Hall

Have you ever thought prayer is useless or wondered if God even hears your prayers? Have you ever thought that because God has much more important matters to take care of, you shouldn't bother to ask for His help with your problems?

Those same thoughts used to invade my mind, but then God took me on a journey, leaving me with absolutely no doubt that He hears our prayers—even the little, seemingly unimportant ones, and He answers them.

I was at church one Sunday with my family, standing next to my husband while we sang the opening hymn at the start of the service. My husband and I like to share the hymnal. He usually holds it, and we always turn slightly toward each other so we can both view the lyrics. We were in this position when a voice popped into my head and said, "See that guy over there?"

Without even thinking, I glanced up. My line of sight brought me to a man standing across the aisle from us, about two rows up. As soon as my eyes made contact with the man, the voice confirmed, "Yes, him."

I answered in my head, "Yes."

The voice then said, "Ask him to lunch."

It was as if someone was standing behind me, talking into my ear and pointing out something to see. It all felt quite natural—until I remembered where I was and what I was doing. I attend church to hear the Word of God, reflect on the message from the hymn, scripture readings, and sermon by the pastor, and attempt to apply what I've learned to my everyday life. So, I ignored the voice as now was not the time to let my mind wander. I kept trying to focus on the hymn to get into the right frame of mind to hear the Word of God. However, the more I attempted to focus my attention, the more the voice persisted with the command, "Ask him to lunch."

I started to question my sanity. I was wondering why this invasive thought persisted despite my attempts to ignore it. There I was at church with my husband, mother, and stepfather, and I was distracted, looking at other men with a strong desire to ask a total stranger out to lunch. What was wrong with me?!

I thought that maybe this was some type of temptation, and I was determined to ignore this ridiculousness.

"Ask him to lunch."

"Ask him to lunch."

I fought this command back with the thought, "I am not going to ask him to lunch. I do not know this man." The congregation is small, and I know most of the people. He did not seem to be with anyone—there was a gap between him and the other people I knew who were near him. Why would I ask him to lunch? Granted, my family and I usually go out to lunch after church, so it would not be difficult or unusual.

"Ask him to lunch."

What if he were to get the wrong idea and think I am asking him on a date?

"Ask him to lunch."

What if my family thinks I am crazy?

"Ask him to lunch."

What if my husband thinks I am flirting with another man?

"Ask him to lunch."

Yes, I will ignore this voice.

"Ask him to lunch."

This was preposterous! There was no way I was going to ask him to lunch! I decided, again, to concentrate on the scripture reading as the lector was reading.

"Ask him to lunch."

Lord, please, I want to hear your Word.

"Ask him to lunch."

I really cannot concentrate with this voice. What is going on?

"Ask him to lunch."

Finally, I could not stand it anymore. I was getting really frustrated. It was like a small child who persists until you finally give them what they want just to get some peace and quiet. "Okay, okay," I relented, "I will ask him out to lunch."

The sudden peace and quiet that overcame me was almost frightening.

After the service, I asked my family if I could invite a man to join us for lunch and pointed him out. Both my mother and my husband asked me if I knew him. I told them no, but I had to ask him to lunch, emphasizing the "had to." Surprisingly, they did not seem to mind at all and agreed that I should go ahead and invite him along. Well, that was easier than I thought it was going to be, but then came the hard part.

I was able to work my way over to the gentleman and introduce myself. I gestured toward my family and asked the man if he would like to join us for lunch. The look on his face was utter shock. The smile on my face froze, and I felt awkward. But after an uncomfortable silence, he swallowed and then smiled and said, "I would love to!"

After getting the details of which restaurant we were going to and meeting us there, he finally sat down at the table with us. We went around the table and introduced ourselves by name. When that was out of the way, he said, "I have got to ask why you asked me to lunch?"

My family all pointed to me. I explained that during the service, "A voice popped into my head telling me to look at you and ask you to lunch. The voice was relentless until I finally agreed that I would do it."

The man's eyes suddenly glistened, and he told us that he had just finished praying for a friend before the start of the service. Now, our eyes watered too, and I realized I was not crazy; God had used me to answer this man's prayer.

He went on to tell us why he was in need of friendship. He had recently converted to Christianity from Judaism, and his conversion was causing problems with his family, particularly in his marriage. His story was amazing.

He had found a flyer from a local Christian church with the service times in his kitchen drawer. He knew this flyer was nothing short of miraculous. It could not have been placed there by anyone in his Jewish family. He took the flyer as a sign, and he began attending Christian services. Soon thereafter, he was on fire with the Holy Spirit and began to find out all he could about Jesus. After much serious research and discernment, he converted to Christianity. Unfortunately, his family became very upset with him, causing him great distress. He was very sad and felt torn between his new love of Jesus Christ and his love for his family. That is why he was praying for a friend. He needed support during this trying time.

Shortly after our luncheon day, we saw him at church, and he invited us to a Seder dinner he was hosting at a Christian church in the area. We accepted the invitation. I accepted because I knew he needed friendship, and we did enjoy his company. My husband accepted as soon as he heard that they would be serving his favorite meat—lamb. However, we had no idea what a Seder dinner was, although our new friend had briefly explained it was the meal served when Jews celebrated Passover.

On the night of the Seder dinner, we entered the Christian church hall where we were welcomed and ushered to a table. At the center of the table was a plate containing symbolic foods. Our friend briefly described the items and explained how the dinner would progress. My mother was chosen to light the candle and say the blessing. I couldn't help but think of a scene from one of my favorite movies, *Fiddler on the Roof*. Exodus, the story in the Bible of the Israelites being freed from slavery in Egypt, was read. It was particularly touching when, as the tenth plague was read, people with real lambs, goats, and sheep made their way through the back of the room. Hearing the bleats from the animals made you feel as if you were experiencing the Exodus story firsthand. Then we sang songs and enjoyed the fellowship.

We couldn't help but reflect that Jesus celebrated the Passover, too. Most Christians are familiar with the last time Jesus celebrated the Passover meal with his disciples before His own crucifixion, what we often refer to as "the last supper." (See Mark 14:12-26). Not only did Jesus *celebrate* Passover, but through His death, Jesus *became* our *true* paschal lamb who suffered for our sins to give us eternal life. This connection from Judaism to Christianity enriched our faith and helped us understand how our friend converted from Judaism to Christianity. The evening was such a blessing. Our friendship did not last long as our new friend soon moved away after accepting a job in another state, but our passing in time was no accident and served us both.

Looking back, I wondered why this happened to me. Try as I might, I am not a saint. However, I was in the right place at the right time to be an answer to a man's prayer. A prayer that God answered as soon as it was uttered. I felt blessed to be an answer to a prayer, and in return, God blessed us all with faith and fellowship. The event strengthened my prayer life and my faith, which increased my gratitude.

Jesus makes it clear in the Bible that we should pray. Even though God knows what we need before we ask (Matthew 6:8), He still wants us to ask. He also wants us to trust God and seek His will. Not our will, but His will. He knows what is best for us. Saint Paul reminds us, *Rejoice always, pray continually, give thanks in all circumstances; for this is God's will for you in Christ Jesus.* (1 Thessalonians 5:16-18 NIV)

Now, you may not know how to pray, and that's okay. As Christians, we are continually growing and learning. And even the disciples needed help praying. They asked Jesus, *"Lord, teach us to pray, just as John taught his disciples." He said to them, "When you pray, say: 'Father, hallowed be your name, your kingdom come. Give us each day our daily bread. Forgive us our sins, for we also forgive everyone who sins against us. And lead us not into temptation.'"* (Luke 11:1-4 NIV) Christians readily recognize this prayer as the Lord's Prayer.

It teaches us that God should come first in our lives, and we are to praise Him, accept His will, ask Him for what we need, confess our sins, forgive others and request His help to overcome temptations from Satan.

Jesus also told us that we should persevere in prayer, saying, *"Ask and it will be given you; seek, and you will find; knock, and the door will be opened to you."* (Matthew 7:7 NIV) The translation from the original language would be more accurate if stated, *ask over and over again,* keep seeking, and don't stop knocking. God wants us to come to Him persistently.

Jesus instructs us further to pray in His name, and He promises us great things when we do. *"Very truly I tell you, whoever believes in me will do the works I have been doing, and they will do even greater things than these, because I am going to the Father. And I will do whatever you ask in my name, so that the Father may be glorified in the Son. You may ask me for anything in my name, and I will do it. If you love me, keep my commands. And I will ask the Father, and He will give you another advocate to help you and be with you forever."* (John 14:12-16 NIV)

The advocate Jesus promised His believers is the Holy Spirit, whom we also have the privilege to call on. In Romans 8:26, Saint Paul tells us, *Likewise the Spirit helps us in our weakness; for we do not know how to pray as we ought, but the Spirit himself intercedes for us with sighs too deep for words.* (RSV) Reflecting on this scripture makes me laugh. I imagine we are sometimes like squirrels running around on a highway, begging and pleading for help. The Holy Spirit hears our pitiful cries and intercedes on our behalf with what could only be expressed as sighs too deep for words accompanied with an eye roll. We need God's help to navigate this life. He is always with us, ready to help when we call. The Holy Spirit helps us to pray as we ought, with reverence. Ask for the Holy Spirit to guide you in prayer.

I can only thank the Holy Spirit for using me to answer a prayer. I imagine He was sighing very deeply when I hesitated to do as He asked. I am thankful to God for bringing me, my family, and this man in need together and blessing us all with a beautiful and joyful experience.

By the way, the hymn we were singing that day was the "Peace Prayer of St. Francis." A hymn sung to God is also a prayer. So even as God answered the silent prayer of the man across the aisle, He also answered the prayer coming from my lips as I sang the words written by the hymn writer: "Lord, make me an instrument of your peace; where there is hatred, let me sow love; where there is injury, pardon; where there is doubt, faith; where there is despair, hope; where there is darkness, light; and where there is sadness, joy. O Divine Master, grant that I may not so much seek to be consoled as to console; to be understood, as to understand; to be loved, as to love; for it is in giving that we receive, it is in pardoning that we are pardoned, and it is in dying that we are born to Eternal Life."

The apostle Paul tells us this: *Do not be anxious about anything, but in every situation, by prayer and petition, with thanksgiving, present your requests to God.* (Philippians 4:6 NIV)

We are all journeying through this life together. And although the world may tell us to be anxious, by praying for ourselves and others, in the name of Jesus and with the guidance of the Holy Spirit, allowing God's will to be done through us, we shall be comforted and blessed with unspeakable joy. I have no doubt.

Joy versus Fear

Have you ever had fears and doubts about what God has called you to do? I know I have. I had huge fears and doubts about being the primary author of this book.

When I was asked in November of 2021 by the founder of Women World Leaders, Kimberly Hobbs, to lead a book project of my choice, I immediately said NO WAY! I felt completely unqualified to do something of this magnitude. She reassured me I was ready and that God had led her and her husband to extend the invitation to me. I agreed to pray about it. The next four months were spent praying about whether God wanted me to write a book and, if so, what I would write about. I was overwhelmed with fear and doubt, convinced I was not qualified.

God does not call the qualified. Instead, He qualifies the called! Look at what God did through Moses, who had been banished to the desert by Pharaoh. Moses was called out of the desert to lead God's people out of bondage and slavery, going up against the powerful Pharaoh of Egypt. Moses didn't know what he was doing, and pleaded with God, saying he was not qualified, he was not a good speaker, and he stuttered—but he became a willing vessel to be used for God's glory! God did the rest!

As I prayed, everywhere I turned, the word Joy kept popping up, coming at me from every angle. I believe God was affirming this mission to me all along, but I was still fearful and doubting. Finally, after praying for almost four months, God directly confirmed to me—while I was praying in the shower!—I was to move forward. And He gave me the titles for these in-between chapter teachings. I had not even agreed to do the book yet, and I certainly did not have any chapter authors yet! I couldn't get out of the shower fast enough to write the titles down. That was the defining moment when I knew I was to move forward with this project, and the title would be *Joy Unspeakable: Regardless of Your Circumstances*. I called Kimberly and told her I would proceed with the book.

Even though I was unqualified, I knew I was to be a willing vessel, and God would do the rest. This was His book, His story, and all for His glory. I made a list of over 30 people whose personal stories could testify to joy. Over 25 originally agreed to participate. Eventually, God weeded out over half of them because it was not His timing. I began to fear and doubt again. But God, in His sovereignty, brought authors from all over the world to share their stories for Him! *Joy Unspeakable!*

I've since learned a lot about joy versus fear.

Joy comes from God's presence *(You will fill me with joy in Your presence.* Psalm 16:11 NIV), and fear is what God delivers us from *(I sought the Lord, and...he delivered me from all my fears.* Psalm 34:4 NIV).

The phrase "fear not" appears 385 times in the Bible, and "do not be afraid" appears 77 times. While the words "joy" and "rejoice" appear over 335 times. God is sending us a message through His book filled with love, hope, peace, and joy: Do not be afraid. Instead, rejoice!

God is the giver of all joy. He is not a God of confusion. He is the same yesterday, today, and forever! (Hebrews 13:8) God does not give us a spirit of fear, but of power and love. (2 Timothy 1:7)

Fears and doubts come from the enemy, who tries to steal our hope, peace, and joy. Fear tries to convince us that all is hopeless. But Romans 5:5 tells us differently. *And hope does not put us to shame, because God's love has been poured out into our hearts through the Holy Spirit, who has been given to us.* (NIV)

So we don't need to fear! Because we can do all God calls us to by harnessing Christ's strength (Philippians 4:13) and holding on to the reality that His power is far greater than that of our enemy. (1 John 4:4)

Jesus reminds us, *I have told you this so that My joy may be in you and that your joy may be complete.* (John 15:11 NIV)

> *May the God of hope fill you with all joy and peace as you trust in Him, so that you may overflow with hope by the power of the Holy Spirit.* (Romans 15:13 NIV)

Joy versus fear? The winner is clear!

. . . .

Elizabeth Anne Bridges

Elizabeth Anne Bridges is one of seven children from an Air Force Family and has traveled the world, even living in England briefly during the Vietnam War with her British-born mother and grandparents. Her two adult children and two stepchildren are her joy.

A graduate of Pembroke Christian Academy in Pembroke Pines, Florida, Elizabeth received a Business Administration degree from Cumberland University in Lebanon, Tennessee. She has worked extensively with human resources, payroll, and time and attendance software implementation for over 20 years. She is a consultant specializing in organization, efficiency, and client relationship management.

Elizabeth enjoys giving books and resources to charitable organizations focusing on young women and children. She posts scriptures and devotions, called Warrior Strong, on social media, encouraging others to know Jesus Christ. She serves in Women World Leaders and United Men of Honor and sends old-fashioned cards to encourage and inspire others to stay strong in Jesus Christ.

Elizabeth loves animals, the symphony, theater, and spending time in museums. She can be contacted at Elizabethwarriorstrong@yahoo.com.

Joy in God's Faithfulness: The Randy and Pam Barton Love Story

by Elizabeth Anne Bridges

We all walk through many seasons in life—from birth to childhood and early adulthood, to marriage, to our final days on this earth. At each stage, we love and are loved. And with each season, we grow, becoming who God created us to be. As we walk, not only can we learn by looking inward and recognizing God's work in our own lives, but we can contemplate and appreciate the lives of others, allowing their actions and attitudes to guide us on our journey. As I consider the lives of Randy and Pam Barton, I see God at work—infusing His unspeakable joy into their lives through ordinary circumstances. And I reflect that I, too, can experience joy amid the ordinary.

> *But the fruit of the Spirit is love, joy, peace, forbearance, kindness, goodness, faithfulness, gentleness and self-control. Against such things there is no law.* (Galatians 5:22-23 NIV)

Randy Barton was a strong magnetic personality who loved God, his family, and the outdoors. *"Anyone who listens to my teaching and follows it is wise, like a person who builds a house on solid rock."* (Matthew 7:24 NLT) He was a Navy veteran who had served his country along with his identical twin Ricky, with whom he was privileged to serve on the same ship. Randy was the type of guy to stop and give a homeless person, usually a veteran like himself, a ride. *"Your love for one another will prove to the world that you are my disciples."* (John 13:35 NLT) He regularly gave money to strangers in need and his love of nature extended to the smallest animals. He often stopped to move turtles to the side of the road. Once, he stopped rush hour traffic in a highly congested area to save a baby duck on the road. Unconcerned for his own safety, he focused on the baby duck. Inspired by his kind actions, others got out of their cars to help as well.

Randy and Ricky loved to sing and play guitars together, performing in Branson, Missouri, harmonizing beautifully together. They even worked with headliner acts such as George Jones and Loretta Lynn.

Randy and his brother became good friends with Amy and Jimmy, a couple who also performed in Branson, and helped them relocate to Tennessee. When Randy asked Amy if she had any friends he might be interested in dating, she named two women. Amy then pulled out a picture of five-year-old Chelsea, explaining that Chelsea was the daughter of her co-worker, Pam. Immediately, Randy said he wanted to date Pam. The two met briefly when Pam brought a crockpot of sloppy joe's over to Amy's new house.

Randy worked hard to get a date with Pam. It took a lot of patience and three to four months of calling to convince her to go out with him. She was a single mom and had been hurt previously, so she was naturally cautious about dating again and avoided his calls. Finally, one day while her parents were visiting, her stepfather answered her phone and handed it to Pam. Randy's patience had finally won, and they set a date for dinner. When Randy arrived at Pam's house, Chelsea ran downstairs to meet her mom's new friend, and they immediately bonded. Pam's heart moved with joy—at that moment, she knew this could be the man God had picked for her.

They were married in a beautiful and simple ceremony at the home of the friends who introduced them. Their wedding photo shows Pam radiant and beautiful, holding a single flower with Randy's arms around her.

> *The steps of a good man are ordered by the Lord, And He delights in his way.* (Psalm 37:23 NKJV)

Randy and Pam built a solid family life together based on their mutual belief in Jesus Christ as Lord and Savior and a desire to serve God as a family. Randy looked for opportunities to serve wherever he could, and Pam joined him in this as opportunities to serve others arose. Together, they counseled one couple who was struggling in their marriage.

Pam was a marketing director at an independent senior living community. She was a beacon of light for residents with the biggest smile and joyful, happy heart. People adored her. Randy was a devoted father to Pam's daughter, Chelsea, whom he loved dearly. Pam and Randy both enjoyed time with family and grilling with friends and neighbors. They saw the importance of investing time and making lasting memories with loved ones.

Randy loved to hunt, spending three weeks each year hunting on the family farm in Missouri, often with his close friend. The farm had sixty acres and a cabin. He brought back lots of venison for family and friends to enjoy. It was his cherished time with God and nature. In addition, it allowed him to see his parents and spend time with his close friend, whom he thought of as a younger brother.

> *How good and pleasant it is when God's people live together in unity!* (Psalm 133:1 NIV)

In October 2020, near the beginning of the COVID pandemic when no vaccines or treatments were available, Randy's twin brother, Ricky, fell ill with COVID and was hospitalized. He was extremely sick, put on a ventilator, and required rehabilitation. They praised God as he fully recovered, and Randy and Pam planned a getaway with Ricky and his wife to celebrate. Time with family was always a priority.

On Valentine's Day, 2021, Pam gave Randy a T-shirt that said, "I love my awesome husband," which they joked about. Life was good. But Randy and Chelsea both felt like they were coming down with a cold. Randy came home from work early a few days later with a backache, thinking it was a kidney stone acting up, and they all decided to get tested for COVID. Pam tested negative, but Chelsea and Randy tested positive. Randy's symptoms worsened, so Pam called his doctor, who prescribed anti-nausea medicine, and confirmed that they were doing everything necessary for his care. But his health did not improve, and Randy asked Pam to take him to the Veterans Hospital emergency room (ER). Due to COVID restrictions, Randy, wearing his pajamas and slippers, had to walk in alone as Pam sat in her car in the parking garage for two hours waiting.

Finally, the ER doctor and nurse FaceTimed (phone video-conferenced) Pam as Randy lay in his bed. He wanted Pam to show the nurse and doctor pictures of his new dog, Timber. She mused that if he was thinking about THAT, well then, he was going to be just fine! The next day the nurse called again; this time, Randy sat in a chair with an oxygen mask on his face. The nurse felt like Randy was ready for some toiletries and gave Pam a list of things to bring to the hospital. Later, Pam FaceTimed Randy again as he was having a protein drink and then again as Randy asked for the checkbook.

Unexpectedly the next day, Pam got a call from the doctor telling her that Randy's oxygen levels were dropping, and he wanted to put Randy on a ventilator. The family's hearts dropped, and intense prayers for healing continued in earnest.

The same day, the doctor and nurse FaceTimed Pam again. Chelsea was beside her as Randy pointed at them and said, "I love you two." They said "I love you" back.

Then later that day, the doctor called Pam again; this time, he told her to come to the hospital immediately. Pam and Chelsea and Ricky and his wife arrived at the hospital. They were led to a family counseling room, where the doctor explained Randy's situation had become dire. The family asked to see him, got suited up in protective clothing, and went to his bedside. Pam was so afraid, watching him slowly start to pass from this world into the arms of Jesus.

> *"Do not let your hearts be troubled. You believe in God; believe also in me. My Father's house has many rooms; if that were not so, would I have told you that I am going there to prepare a place for you? And if I go and prepare a place for you, I will come back and take you to be with me that you also may be where I am. You know the way to the place where I am going."* (John 14:1-4 NIV)

Pam held Randy's hand as they all expressed their love and prayed over him. Then the nurse put her hand on Pam's shoulder, gently telling her Randy's heart had stopped. He was gone from this earth and was beginning his journey home with the Lord.

It was a shocking and distressing moment. Pam had no idea when she took Randy to the hospital that he would not recover. She was grief-stricken and heartbroken, but she knew God was with her.

> *Even when I walk through the darkest valley, I will not be afraid, for you are close beside me. Your rod and staff protect and comfort me.* (Psalm 23:4 NLT)

God continued to bless Pam as she journeyed on without Randy.

Randy had passed away on March 3, 2021, at 12:29 pm. The number 29 has always been significant for Pam as her birthday is January 29, and as the first anniversary of Randy's death approached, she began seeing "29s" everywhere. One night, while walking Timber, she touched her phone to see the time—7:29. She asked herself what all the 29s might mean, and she felt she heard Randy's voice shout, "It means I love you, Pam!" She laughed and cried as she walked, finding comfort in that experience.

A few months after Randy's passing, his close hunting friend and his wife flew in from Maryland to be with Pam and Chelsea. They were such a gift of strength and comfort. God always knows exactly what we need, even when we don't.

> *The Lord is close to the broken-hearted; He rescues those whose spirits are crushed.* (Psalm 34:18 NLT)

As she replayed their last few months together in her head, Pam was struck by how God had blessed and prepared them for what was coming. Randy had even told Pam that when he passed, he wanted to be cremated and have his ashes spread near a big oak tree on the family farm in Missouri, where he hunted.

So when the tender time came to spread Randy's ashes, the family gathered with his ashes in plastic cups and scattered them around the big oak tree and near his favorite hunting stand. Despite the ache in their souls, God went before them, bringing peace and yes, joy, amid the pain as He ensured that the farm looked beautiful that day, with daisies blooming everywhere. Pam was reminded that Randy had always wanted to bring her daisies back from his spring turkey hunting trip but thought they would wilt before he got home. That day, God made sure she experienced the daisies in all their glory.

Pam, Chelsea, Randy's twin brother and his wife, and Randy's parents all took part in the scattering of his ashes. Then, Pam picked daisies and put them in one of the cups they used for ashes. She added water, and they lasted a month. Pam found a little bit of strength in those daisies.

> *Do not be afraid, for I am with you. Don't be discouraged, for I am your God. I will strengthen you and help you. I will hold you up with My victorious right hand.* (Isaiah 41:10 NLT)

As Pam now deals with the various phases of grief, she finds comfort in a small daisy ring she wears daily. She also wears a locket that she had custom-made with Randy's photo and the number 29. The picture reflects Randy's love for God and clearly shows the Holy Spirit shining brightly through him as he sits on a fishing pier with the brilliant sunset behind him. Remembering the love of God that continually flowed from Randy comforts and inspires Pam—just as I pray that gazing into his life inspires you.

Pam recently received a message from Randy's mom that the Clarence Young

Men's Organization of Clarence, Missouri, wanted to put up a veterans sign in Randy's honor. Pam was thrilled, knowing Randy would be very honored as a proud veteran who loved his country.

Grieving is a part of life that we all must experience, but Pam has exhibited how to grieve well.

Walking through grief includes encountering good days filled with laughter and happy memories, along with poignant, precious days filled with tears. Neither is bad. God uses both to cleanse and renew us. As Pam revisited the life she and Randy shared, she reflected on one of their last special moments together—when they had lovingly danced the night away under the Christmas lights on the back deck, which Randy had built as a Mother's Day gift to Pam.

There is joy in knowing God is always faithful. He brings the right memories and people to help carry us through our difficult times. *He comforts us in all our troubles so that we can comfort others. When they are troubled, we will be able to give them the same comfort God has given us.* (2 Corinthians 1:4 NLT)

We often do not think of the loss of a loved one as requiring humility. But it does. It is the realization that we are not in control as Christians or individuals; only God is. We do not get do-overs or second chances, and we must live for God daily in all our words and actions. Both Pam and Randy did that. Were they perfect? No, as none of us are, but they loved God and showed love to each other. Randy left knowing how much his wife, daughter, and family loved and respected him. We cannot take anything for granted. We are ALL here temporarily. God is sovereign and chooses our time to go home. We get to enjoy family, friends, and others until He chooses to take us to heaven. We must love others daily as much as we can, just as Jesus loves us.

But our true knowledge, as Christians who have accepted Jesus Christ as our Savior, is that life is not temporary. We have the joy of knowing that we have eternal life. Our life does not end here on earth. We journey to our perfect home when we pass from here to heaven to be with God, our Creator. So yes, it is hard for those of us left behind since we no longer see our loved ones day-to-day, but the realization is that we will see them again at our appointed time in heaven with Jesus. *And this is the way to have eternal life—to know You, the only true God, and Jesus Christ, the One You sent to earth.* (John 17:3 NLT)

As we reflect on our suffering during any season of loss, we must understand we have a perfect Creator who understands our grief more than we know. He watched as His Son was humiliated, beaten, and cruelly treated on the road to the cross and crucifixion. He watched as His Son was nailed to the cross by His hands and feet. He saw incredible pain as Jesus was lifted on the cross, and His body hung with the weight on those pierced Holy hands and feet. God watched as His Son languished in pain and suffered until it was His appointed time to die. So, He knows our pain perfectly as our loved ones pass into heaven. He fully understands our grief. God's love and Jesus' submission to death consumed our sins and our pain long before we suffered our losses. He loved us first. He carries us in our journeys of life, through all the amazing ups and downs we endure. That is our humility. He does not ask us to do what He already did first. He overcame death for us.

> *We love each other because He loved us first.* (1 John 4:19 NLT) *We do this by keeping our eyes on Jesus, the champion who initiates and perfects our faith. Because of the joy awaiting him, he endured the cross, disregarding its shame. Now he is seated in the place of honor beside God's throne.* (Hebrews 12:2 NLT)

Because of our belief in Jesus Christ as our Lord and Savior, we have eternal life. *For this is how God loved the world: He gave His one and only Son, so that everyone who believes in him will not perish but have eternal life.* (John 3:16 NLT) While our earthly bodies may die, our spirits ascend to heaven, another part of God's creation where we will live eternally. Our loved ones are not dead; they are alive in Spirit. And in God's great mercy, He reminds us through nature and signs that they are still with us and in our hearts, bringing us deep-seated joy.

Joy - A Fruit of the Spirit

The Fruit of the Spirit consists of nine different characteristics of God: love, joy, peace, patience, kindness, goodness, faithfulness, gentleness, and self-control. (Galatians 5:22-23) All are expressions of the Lord Jesus Christ within us. Fruit is the supernatural result of being filled with the Holy Spirit. It is proof that the Spirit of God lives within us, and having it depends on our connection to the presence of the Lord, especially in times of hardship.

Joy is one of the fruits of the Spirit. It's one thing to have joy when God is pouring out His blessings on us, but it is a supernatural choice to *Rejoice in the Lord always* (Philippians 4:4 NIV), especially in times of struggle. How we act when the chips are down is our testimony. People watch us all the time, and they pay close attention to how we respond in a crisis. Do we completely fall apart in our plight, or do we handle our predicament with joy and peace beyond all comprehension?

We can bear the fruit of the Spirit by abiding in Him. We abide in Him by being obedient—by loving God and keeping His commandments. How do we grow in love for God? As we get to know Him more and more every day, we will naturally fall in love with Him. And we can get to know Him more by spending time reading His Word and in worship, fellowship, and prayer. The more we know Him, the more we love Him, and the more we obey Him. The more we obey Him, the more we abide in Him. The more we abide in Him, the more fruit we bear for Him, and the more joy and peace we experience in good times and bad.

God wants us to bear much fruit, including joy. In John 15:4-5, Jesus told His disciples in the upper room, *"Remain in Me, as I also remain in you. No branch can bear fruit by itself; it must remain in the vine. Neither can you bear fruit unless you remain in me. I am the vine; you are the branches. If you remain in me and I in you, you will bear much fruit; apart from me you can do nothing."* (NIV)

Jesus, full of joy yet knowing His crucifixion was imminent, continued telling the disciples in John 15:11, *"I have told you this so that my joy may be in you and that your joy may be complete."* (NIV)

What was His joy? It was the Resurrection! He looked through the cross and saw what we couldn't see—the resurrection and eternal life for you and me! He didn't focus on the cross; His focus was on us. Because of the joy set before Him, He endured the cross. (Hebrews 12:2) While Jesus was on the cross, you were on His mind!

We must look beyond our current circumstances and see Jesus' joy. Fix your eyes on the unseen, because what is seen is temporary, but what is unseen is eternal. (2 Corinthians 4:18 NIV)

Think of JOY as an acronym for Jesus, Others, Yourself. Do everything you do for Jesus and for the good of others, and you will reap and experience bountiful Joy!

. . . .

Anja Cook

Originally from South Africa, Anja moved to Australia 10 years ago and resides on the Gold Coast with her three children. As a family, they love spending time in nature and going camping. Their goal is to purchase a property where they can plant a veggie garden and have chickens and other animals.

Anja is the director of a Classical Conversations homeschool community on the Gold Coast. When she's not busy homeschooling, she's also an avid entrepreneur. She has owned a bridal boutique in South Africa and, more recently, a stainless-steel peg business in Australia. She also runs an organic loose-leaf tea business and is a shampoo dealer for a multi-billion-dollar hair and skin care company.

She is passionate about equipping stay-at-home mums and women who have come out of a domestic violence relationship to gain confidence and walk in the purposes God has for them. She is a big advocate against domestic violence and the porn industry.

In her spare time, Anja enjoys running long distances, going to the beach or creek, writing poetry, or reading a good book.

Her dream is to see women who have been through abuse come out the other end healed, restored, full of joy, and in a thriving relationship with Christ. She believes that God can heal past hurts. He can make whole the person who has been physically or emotionally broken.

There is a joyful life waiting for you.

Joy Restored
By Anja Cook

As a little girl, my mum always referred to me as her little ray of sunshine. Even one of my teachers said I should smile often because I had the most beautiful smile.

And as an adult, I did. I smiled and pretended that everything was okay. I put on the mask of contentment and kept going as though everything was just fine. I brushed off snarky remarks in front of friends and bit my tongue. I gracefully held my head high when I was told to get changed because what I was wearing was supposedly not suitable. I held my poise and carried on. I learnt the art of treading on eggshells without breaking any. I considered myself a 'good wife,' an aspiring Proverbs 31 wife, but I felt I would never be good enough.

A few years ago, my dream of living a happily-ever-after life shattered when my marriage of 10 years came to an end. It had been a long time coming with infidelity, addiction, and endless emotional, psychological, and sexual abuse. Thinking back, I should have left years earlier, but faith kept me there. I kept trusting, kept praying that somehow, something would change. I trusted God that He would do a good work in my husband. I trusted that the abuse would stop. I prayed and asked God what needed to change in me. I tried to do all the right things, say all the right things, and not do the things that could potentially cause an explosion. However, nothing I did worked. I ended up a nervous wreck, fearing a man who was meant to love me more than I feared God. That's when I knew I had to get out.

I grew up in a Christian home, and divorce wasn't ever an option, no matter how hard things got. I didn't know what abuse looked like or even that I was in an abusive relationship. It was simply not in my frame of reference and also not something I ever talked about with my girlfriends, let alone my parents. I slowly found myself more fearful of a person than having a reverent fear of the God who loved me most. I knew God loved me, and I loved Him and had a good relationship with Him. I went to Bible study and church. I read the Word and prayed and worshipped. However, something was missing. I had lost my identity in Christ. I didn't see my worth as a child of the most high King. Even though I knew the insults and accusations flung at me were lies, they still broke me. They say that "sticks and stones may break my bones, but words can never hurt me." Well, 'they' were wrong. Proverbs 18:21 says that *Death and life are in the power of the tongue.* (NKJV) I felt like I had death spoken over me for far too long. I was running on empty.

On the first Christmas morning after the separation from my long-time marriage partner, God re-awakened the joy inside me, the joy I had as a little girl. I woke up with the song "I Am Free" by the Newsboys in my heart.

I truly was free, or so I thought. There was no longer anyone telling me what to wear, accusing me of things I didn't do, or coercing me to do things I didn't want to do. I didn't constantly have to think whether I was doing something wrong or whether I had said the right thing. But if I had known that morning what was lying ahead, I probably wouldn't have grasped hold of that joy so easily. I might have even chosen to sit in the sorrow or drown in my tears. Thankfully I didn't know, and the joy I received that morning, no one and nothing could take away from me. A little piece was added to the joy puzzle.

Most people think that when you leave an abusive relationship, it's over—the abuse magically disappears, and you can carry on with your life as normal. When you are being abused, many people ask, "why doesn't she just leave?" Sadly, most people don't realise that when you separate from an abusive marriage, the abuse doesn't just cease. On the contrary, it intensifies more than you could imagine. It twists your mind, making you think you would've been better off staying and sucking it up. The anger or hatred towards you is exacerbated, like pouring fuel on a fire. Then the abused is further ravaged by court case after court case, little remarks here and there, tainted children's views of their protective parent—the list goes on. Additionally, there are multiple interviews where you have to relive the trauma or try to work through the trauma by telling your story over and over to counsellors. Then comes the doubting and the self-reproach. "Did this really happen?" "How did I even get here?" "How was I so ignorant?" "What's wrong with me?" "How could I let this happen?" "Why didn't I leave sooner?"

It takes a strong person to walk away from an abusive relationship. It takes a strong person to fight for their children whilst having to provide for them financially, look after their emotional well-being, and keep it together. It takes a strong person not to run away from God—or even blame Him—and fall into the hand of the world. I am not a strong person, but Christ is strong in me. *"The JOY of the LORD is your strength."* (Nehemiah 8:10 NKJV) His JOY has kept me strong. It is His JOY that has kept me going when I felt like giving up. And it is His JOY that helped me feel a little less broken and a little more like the person He created me to be.

> *You have turned for me my mourning into dancing; You have put off my sackcloth and clothed me with gladness...I will give thanks to You forever.* (Psalm 30:11-12 NKJV)

I think one of the keys to being joyful is giving thanks. Try saying thank you for something while you're angry. It's not possible, or at least it won't be genuine. No matter how big or how small, one cannot give thanks to the Lord without a teeny, tiny bit of joy igniting inside of you. Hopefully, it's a huge burst of joy.

During my time of recovery, whenever I fell into the trap of self-pity, I would remember where I used to be and thank God for the current trial, knowing I was one step further away from where I used to be. I was no longer in the house with an abusive husband, and I knew the endless court cases would have to come to an end at some point. There were times when horrible things would come at me, and sometimes only later, I would see how God worked those situations for good. I can look back at those trials now with so much thankfulness.

Romans 8:28 says: *And we know that all things work together for good to those who love God, to those who are the called according to His purpose.* (NKJV)

Not long after the separation, I bought myself a new notebook. The cover reads, "Whoever is happy will make others happy too." - quote by Anne Frank. I say whoever is joyful will overflow and make others joyful too. Happiness is fleeting. It is an emotion, like sadness and anger. We are not responsible for others' happiness. However, joy is more than a feeling. It is something that bursts inside of you, like a fountain. It is something breathed inside of you by our heavenly Father as we give Him praise, glory, and honour. I can be happy about the sunny weather or sad about the thunderstorm that ruined the event, but when I have joy, I can celebrate regardless of the circumstances.

Writing used to be something that made me happy. I used to love writing all sorts of poems and short stories. But for a very long time, I couldn't pick up a pen and write. Even writing this story, *my story*, has been incredibly hard. It was like the creative part of my brain had shut down from all the trauma.

I had constantly been living in a state of fight or flight, survival of the fittest. Some days I just went through the motions to get through another day. And when I did have time for a breather, I would find something to keep me busy so that I didn't have to sit with my thoughts and emotions. That's trauma for you. (Thankfully, I have had some good counsellors and friends encourage me to sit with the uncomfortable feelings. I also serve a gracious God who is constantly healing the broken bits and pieces and bringing me to the fullness of joy.)

About a year into the separation, I picked up my pen. God started dropping little poems into my head, and I couldn't find my notebook quickly enough to write them down. Sometimes I would just make a note on my phone or, if I didn't have my phone on me, I would repeat the line over and over so that I wouldn't forget it and write it down later. Another piece of the joy puzzle was coming back.

Slowly but surely, I started discovering who I was, what I liked, and what I disliked. It was like I was becoming a whole new person. After the separation, I felt so empty inside—like my identity and everything I had were ripped apart. Still, I really struggled to come to terms with what had happened to me. For so long, I didn't recognize I was living in an abusive marriage. I didn't understand that one could even be sexually abused in a marriage. I felt absolutely worthless. I felt that I wasn't worthy of a lot of things. I even wondered what I had done to deserve this. *What was wrong with me? How did I lose my fear of God and fear another person more?* I was ashamed. I was worried about what others would think of me, and I wondered who would ever love someone with so little self-worth that they ended up like this. I wondered how someone could ever love me and my kids.

You see, the enemy can have a field day with us when we don't find our identity and our joy in the one true living God.

I had to remember or rediscover what I loved. I had to make an effort to find myself instead of just being a wife and a mum. I found joy in writing, even if it was just every other month or when the inspiration struck. I found joy in nature and spending lazy afternoons by the creek with my kids.

I had to rediscover my style. I used to enjoy wearing floral patterns and bright colours. As time progressed, my wardrobe became a little more black and plain, and I was also very limited with what I was able to spend on clothing. On occasion, I was told what to wear and where I had to shop. I not only lost my identity inside, but I also lost my identity on the outside.

After the separation, I had to figure out what clothing I liked and what shoes I preferred. I started making an effort with my hair again and putting on a bit more makeup. One time a friend blessed me with some money. I was so overwhelmed by her generosity. I knew I had to put some of it towards bills, but I strongly felt I should go shopping and try on some dresses. I wasn't used to buying myself anything I didn't absolutely need. As I shopped, I felt so out of place, almost as if everyone was watching me. Eventually, I found 'the one' and clearly heard God say that I am His beloved daughter and worthy of wearing a pretty dress. I had been diminished into the mentality that I wasn't worth it and should only spend my money on the bare necessities. If I had anything extra, I would use it on my kids. But not this time. This time I bought a dress, not because I needed it, but because I was worth it. Another piece of the joy puzzle was restored.

I vividly remember the first time I bought myself new bedding, finding joy in decorating my room and my house. I bought and sold furniture to make some extra money to be able to afford what I liked. Something that would seem so mundane to many brought me so much joy. It wasn't about being materialistic, but it was about creating a home where I could find peace and joy. Looking around my house, I could see His provision everywhere. I could see all the people who had helped me move or pick up a piece of furniture; I was so blessed and overjoyed. Another piece of the puzzle, restored.

Still, there was this one missing piece, this longing, this hope that one day I could experience what a godly marriage is all about. Perhaps one day, I would be able to live the life I had dreamed of—not a fairytale, but a marriage where man and woman are created equal, where they love and honour one another, and where Christ truly is at the centre. Yet, even if this is not His plan for me, His presence is enough. I am encouraged by the words in Psalm 16:9-11(NKJV):

> *Therefore my heart is glad, and my glory rejoices;*
> *My flesh also will rest in hope.*
> *For You will not leave my soul in Sheol,*
> *Nor will You allow Your Holy One to see corruption.*
> *You will show me the path of life;*
> *In Your presence is fullness of joy;*
> *At Your right hand are pleasures forevermore.*

The scripture in Romans 12:12 has been another great encouragement for me: *rejoicing in hope, patient in tribulation, continuing steadfastly in prayer.* (NKJV)

I rejoice in the hope that I will be completely restored from my brokenness and that God has a plan for my life. It has been hard being patient in this time of tribulation. So many times, I have asked God for the court cases to just come to an end so that I can carry on with a somewhat normal life. Only God knows when it will finally come to an end, but I know that through it all, His JOY is my strength. Prayer has been the thing that has kept me steadfast in Him. And I can truly testify of the many, *many* times He has answered my prayers and the prayers of those around me who are petitioning God for my situation. Wow, we serve an incredibly faithful God. My story is not over. God is continually adding and restoring pieces to my joy puzzle.

My hope is that if someone or something has stolen your joy or you are currently facing trials that feel like never-ending mountains, you will find the true joy that only comes from the Father. Don't look for happiness. It won't stick around. Don't try to find joy in a partner or a pet or a spending spree or a lotto ticket or a one-night stand. Happiness doesn't last, and it certainly won't carry you through trials and tribulations.

> *Though the fig tree may not blossom,*
> *Nor fruit be on the vines;*
> *Though the labor of the olive may fail,*
> *And the fields yield no food;*
> *Though the flock may be cut off from the fold,*
> *And there be no herd in the stalls—*
> *Yet I will rejoice in the Lord,*
> *I will joy in the God of my salvation.*
> *The Lord God is my strength;*
> *He will make my feet like deer's feet,*
> *And He will make me walk on my high hills.*
> (Habakkuk 3:17-19 NKJV)

I pray that your joy is restored to the point of overflowing. May you be so filled with joy that it is contagious to those around you. I pray you will find strength in the joy of the Lord.

I recently found a note on my phone. I can't remember whether someone shared it with me in prayer or whether it was preached on a Sunday, but the note reads:

"What you thought you could only heal through pain, I can heal through JOY."

I leave you with Isaiah 49:13 (NKJV):

> *Sing, O heavens! Be joyful, O earth! And break out in singing, O mountains! For the LORD has comforted His people, And will have mercy on His afflicted.*

Joy in Who He Says We Are

When you stop amid the craziness of life and allow God to speak to your heart, you are quickly reminded by the nudging of the Holy Spirit of who you are in Christ. The reality is that Jesus, who died on the cross for us because of His love for you and me, speaks incredible words over our lives. There is such peace and joy in knowing who we are in Him. To know that we exist because of Jesus is beyond humbling. Oh, how undeserving we are to receive this kind of love and acceptance.

We are God's creations. And the beautiful thing about this is that we no longer need to strive to be more. We are enough, just as He created us. Psalm 139:13-16 beautifully says, *For you formed my inward parts; you knitted me together in my mother's womb. I praise you, for I am fearfully and wonderfully made. Wonderful are your works; my soul knows them very well. My frame was not hidden from you, when I was being made in secret, intricately woven in the depths of the earth. Your eyes saw my unformed substance; in your book were written, every one of them, the days that were formed for me, when as yet there was none of them.* (ESV)

No one knows us better or loves us more than God does.

As you walk your journey in life, consistently remind yourself who you are in Jesus.

You are chosen.
You are accepted.

You are enough.
You are redeemed.
You are whole.
You are beautiful.
You are God's beloved.
You are a child of the King.

Your heavenly Father loves you just as you are. Nothing in your life takes Him by surprise. We should constantly remind ourselves of the joy we bring Him by just being who He created us to be. There is beautiful joy in placing our identity in Jesus.

Finding joy in whom God says we are takes intentionality—because the enemy would love nothing more than for us to stay in a defeated place. But God wants us to take captive the thoughts which are contrary to His love and, instead, let His true words about our identity sink into the depths of our soul. God gives us a priceless gift to be His sons and daughters. That is the best identity ever.

Walking boldly with our heads held high in whom He created us to be is the best gift we can offer Jesus. The words we speak over ourselves can have the most impact on how we see ourselves. The last thing we want to do is to disappoint the Creator of the universe as we tell Him that He made a mistake by creating us the way He did. There are no mistakes when it comes to Jesus. He is sovereign, and His love for us is everlasting.

Take a moment to allow the joy of being a creation of God sink into the crevices of your heart. Enjoying your identity in Him will surely bring a smile to your Creator's face.

Louisa van der Westhuizen

Louisa comes from South Africa and grew up in Cape Town, in the shadow of the iconic Table Mountain. Today she lives in Stellenbosch, in the Cape Winelands, surrounded by magnificent mountains and flora.

After school, she was unsure which career she should pursue and ended up doing a B.Sc-degree with Biochemistry and Microbiology as her Major subjects. She knew that her chances of a career with a degree in science would be better than with a B.A., although she loves languages and other B.A. subjects. She first obtained an Honours degree in Microbiology and subsequently also a Master's degree in Microbiology while doing research on malo-lactic bacteria in wine. She and her husband met at a Student Christian movement camp. They married, were blessed with a son and a daughter, and now have six wonderful grandchildren, each with their own special personalities and endearing characteristics. As a full-time mother for 18 years, she learned that engaging with and helping other people was her actual God-given passion. Returning to work, she was fortunate to be involved with preparing practical classes for the students, interacting with them, and helping them to understand difficult concepts.

Louisa loves reading, music, choir singing, ballet, gardening, and running half and full marathons. God has blessed her with perseverance, which perhaps explains her love of long-distance running. Living in Stellenbosch allows her to be out in His creation and, when running on her own, to spend time with Him.

MY WALK WITH GOD THROUGH CANCER

By Louisa van der Westhuizen

> *Not unto us, O LORD, not unto us, but unto thy name give glory, for thy mercy, and for thy truth's sake.* (Psalm 115:1 KJV)

My journey with cancer started long before I knew it. One evening, my breast suddenly felt as though I was a mom who should have breastfed her baby an hour or more ago. I looked down and saw that the nipple was slightly inverted. The next morning, Friday, the third of August 2018, I immediately called to schedule a mammogram. The first available appointment was the following Wednesday. A colleague suggested I contact the surgeon to see whether he could expedite the process. The surgeon just asked to see me the day before the mammogram to determine whether a biopsy was necessary.

Assured by the words, *The LORD makes firm the steps of the one who delights in Him.* (Psalm 37:23 NIV), I went for my Saturday morning long run—I am a runner of half marathons (21.1km). My son had challenged me to attempt the Two Oceans Ultra Marathon (56km), described as the world's most beautiful marathon, with him in 2019 as it would be the fiftieth one.

At my appointment on Tuesday, the surgeon didn't say anything to alarm me, but he did authorise a biopsy. Then on Wednesday, I went for the mammogram and biopsy and was told the surgeon would only get the results on Monday because of a public holiday.

The next Tuesday morning, before 08:00, I received a call that I was to meet with the surgeon at 17:00 that day. Despite this, I was not perturbed because I knew I was in the hands of my Heavenly Father. *A father is tender and kind to his children. In the same way, the Lord is tender and kind to those who have respect for him.* (Psalm 103:13 NIRV) *They will have no fear of bad news; their hearts are steadfast, trusting in the Lord.* (Psalm 112:7 NIV) My only concern was that I had a Time Trial to run at 18:00, which would make for a tight schedule.

I sat in the surgeon's office as he explained what he saw on the mammogram and sonar. Then, he said straight out: "It's cancer." I am still in awe of God's unimaginable grace—as I sat there, I felt no fear. This news was merely part of my journey, and I knew God would be there with me all the way. *So do not fear, for I am with you; do not be dismayed, for I am your God. I will strengthen you and help you; I will uphold you with my righteous right hand.* (Isaiah 41:10 NIV)

The surgeon explained that I had a Lobular Carcinoma, which meant there was no lump, but cancer invaded and spread through my breast tissue like fingers. It was not an aggressive tumor and had probably been there since the previous year. Since it is not easy to detect because of the way that it invades the tissue, it was likely that it might not have been detected previously. The problem was that the tumor was very large (5cm), and at least three lymph nodes showed indications of being cancerous, classifying it as Stage 3. There are only four stages of cancer; the fourth is often fatal. The surgeon immediately scheduled a total mastectomy ten days later. The surgery would include pectoral muscles, axillary and internal mammary lymph nodes. I had to go for an MRI scan the next day to ascertain whether the cancer had spread to any other parts of my body. Needless to say, I was not on time for the Time Trial.

That evening, I told my daughter in Australia the news. My son was away on a business trip and I did not want to distract him while he was in meetings where he needed to concentrate. The next day was my daughter-in-law's birthday, so I held back on telling them. When I informed my son, it was with the declaration, "But we are still doing Oceans next year."

By Thursday midday, I phoned the surgeon's receptionist to inquire about the results of the MRI scan. She informed me that he was seeing patients the whole day and operating from 17:00, but might have time to phone me in between. That evening our Bible study group met at our house and prayed for me. By then, I wondered why the surgeon could not have just left me a message. Was it bad news that he had to convey to me personally? A miraculous calm descended on me. I knew that if my cancer had spread and I was not going to make it, this was part of my journey with God and He would be there all the way. *Be anxious for nothing, but in everything by prayer and supplication, with thanksgiving, let your requests be made known to God; and the peace of God, which surpasses all understanding, will guard your hearts and minds through Christ Jesus.* (Philippians 4:6-7 NKJV)

Looking back, I can hardly believe that I was so ready to face death if that was part of God's journey for me. This truly was a supernatural peace. When we had nearly finished drinking tea after our Bible study and prayer, the surgeon called. He had just stepped out of the operating theatre, and although it was late, he wanted to inform me that the rest of my body was clean. I was immensely grateful. As my friends waved goodbye, I gave them a thumbs-up.

I am a microbiologist and was employed at the University of Stellenbosch as a technical assistant, preparing practical classes for students. I immediately set to work preparing ahead any general items I could. Unfortunately, that semester's course was one where the students did real research, and one could only prepare weekly as their projects evolved. I was optimistic that I might be back after two weeks. Fortunately, the lecturer stepped in and divided my work amongst my colleagues. *Many are the plans in a person's heart, but it is the Lord's purpose that prevails.* (Proverbs 19:21 NIV)

Continuing my training, I was grateful to complete a five-kilometer Time Trial the Tuesday before my operation in less than 25 minutes. This meant so much to me as I would probably not be running for quite some time

A day before the operation, my husband and I went to the hospital to sign documents and make the necessary payments. I was informed I would need to have pajamas that could be unbuttoned in front to facilitate getting dressed and undressed. I suddenly realized that all my pajamas were without buttons. My friend, who took me to the hospital the next day, altered an oversized pair I bought on sale. Another friend went to great lengths to find me a pair of pajamas in another town, about a 20-minute drive from Stellenbosch. *Therefore take no thought, saying, What shall we eat? Or, What shall we drink? Or, Wherewithal shall we be clothed? (For after all these things do the Gentiles seek:) for your heavenly Father knoweth that ye have need of all these things.* (Matthew 6:31-32 KJV)

On the day of my surgery, my friend sat with me in the foyer for over an hour while I waited to be admitted. Even the anesthesiologist was irritated that the staff neglected to get me in my room and ready, but he put my mind to rest that there was still enough time and everything would go smoothly. When I woke up from surgery, I was uncomfortable and in pain. The surgeon had needed to cut into muscle to remove the required one-centimeter clean tissue around the tumor. Additionally, I had a bag attached to my wound to drain fluid, restricting my movement. Sleeping was also fairly uncomfortable. It was a blessing to have friends come and visit me. One friend brought me two pairs of pajamas, and another brought me a bar of special lavender soap with no chemical additives or artificial perfume, which can stimulate the growth of cancerous cells.

After the pathology tests came back, my cancer was classified as Stage 3B.

Typically, people have approximately 12 axillary lymph nodes; I had 27, and 19 of those tested positive for cancer.

I was finally discharged after the fluid draining from the wound dropped to a specific minimum per day. God sent angels to watch over me. I had scarcely arrived home when my daughter-in-law and her mother arrived with enough food for the freezer for at least two weeks. As we walked out to the car, I picked up a cerise pink feather. I'd lost a friend just a month before to whom feathers had a special meaning. I knew this was a message from my deceased friend and God. *He shall cover thee with His feathers, and under His wings shalt thou trust: His truth shall be thy shield and buckler.* (Psalm 91:4 KJV)

Friends offered to shop for me, help me get the washing on the line, and one friend with a cleaning service fetched my washing and brought it back ironed. Another friend took me for my follow-up appointment with the surgeon.

The surgeon knew I wasn't very enthusiastic about chemotherapy, having read about its detrimental effects and also about alternative therapies. He wanted me to see the oncologist and listen to her with an open mind. So I went, and God graciously provided a friend who had traveled the same path many years before to accompany me. The oncologist explained the gravity of the situation and gave me some reading matter on what to expect. I was to receive four treatments with fluorouracil, also known as 5FU, epirubicin (a red fluid known as the red devil because of its side effects), and cyclophosphamide. These were to be followed by four more of the "lighter" version of chemotherapy, namely docetaxel.

My treatment was to occur at three weekly intervals. I had to go to the pathologists the day before each treatment to ascertain whether my white blood cell count, an indication of my immune system's health, was high enough. Chemotherapy depletes your white blood cells; if my white blood cell count was too low, I would have to wait a week before being tested again.

In the meantime, my colleagues at work said that they didn't want me to come back before the student practical classes were over, as they were working with organisms that could be detrimental to my health because of my compromised immune system. My surgeon willingly declared me to be unfit for work for the extra weeks.

At each treatment session, the chemotherapy drugs were separately administered intravenously in my forearm, taking 2-3 hours. Then, it took another half an hour or so while they flushed the vein with saline to get rid of the concentrated chemotherapy fluid. My mastectomy was on the left side, so the drugs were injected into my right arm, forcing me to rest it on the armrest with an ice pack to try to prevent it from burning. If I wanted to go to the toilet, I had to take the drip with me and could only use my left hand. I developed a headache and a bit of nausea but took ginger biscuits and lozenges to counteract that. I also received a Neulastim injection, which I administered abdominally after 24 hours so that it did not interfere with the chemotherapy. This would stimulate my immune system, boosting my white blood cell count so that I could receive the next treatment in three weeks' time. Later I found out that the Neulastim contributed to the terrible headaches I was getting after each session. I also started to develop an aversion to ginger lozenges and ginger tea. My friend who had been down the same path warned me not to wear my favorite perfume or take along my favorite snack as I might also develop an aversion to those.

After my first chemotherapy session, I ran a 10km race. The oncologist encouraged me to keep running as her fit patients handled the treatment the best. I had to walk when my heart rate went up too much, an indication I was overexerting myself, which could cause me to not be ready for the next chemotherapy session. Although I walked quite a stretch to lower my heart rate, I still finished in less than an hour. Tears welled up in my eyes when I crossed the finish line as the third Grand Master (60-69). I felt so blessed.

I was so elated with this accomplishment that it didn't even bother me when I started losing clumps of hair the next morning. I immediately thought of the possibility of having curly hair when it grew back. Over the weeks to come, I would realize how many hairs we have, as they just kept falling out. My hairdresser cut it when it became patchy. My pillow was still covered in short hairs every morning. I marveled at the fact that it says in the Bible: *Aren't two sparrows sold for only a penny? But not one of them falls to the ground outside your Father's care. He even counts every hair on your head! So don't be afraid. You are worth more than many sparrows.* (Matthew 10:29-31 NIRV) It was amazing to think that God counted every one of those thousands of hairs falling out over a period of more than a month.

After my second chemotherapy session, I realized that the Two Oceans Ultra Marathon would not happen. Participants have to run a qualifying marathon in less than five hours, and during a half marathon, I walked so much to keep my heart rate down that it took me three hours to complete. My son and I decided we would rather attempt the half marathon the next year, which would also be special as it would be my tenth one, earning me a permanent number no one else would ever be able to use. *We know that all things work together for the good of those who love God, who are called according to His purpose.* (Romans 8:28 CSB)

As the treatment progressed, my nausea, headaches, and the metallic taste in my mouth increased. I was also taking longer to recover. In the end, I was barely feeling myself before the next treatment. Despite all this, God gave me a supernatural fountain of joy in my heart, which I wanted to share with others as much as I could. *The one who believes in me, as the Scripture has said, will have streams of living water flow from deep within him.* (John 7:38 CSB)

After the fifth treatment, which was supposed to be the lighter version, I was feeling a bit weak while we prepared to visit friends at the seaside, four hours from home. Shortly after our arrival, I started to feel ill. I had a constant stomach ache, and my whole body ached. By the next day, I developed a fever. That evening my husband took me to the emergency room of the nearest hospital. I was given an injection to ease the pain, but the doctor would not admit me as I was at risk of infection by any organisms in the hospital. God provided for my needs. My friend of 62 years, who lived near the seaside resort, came home with us. After a few days of my getting worse, she took me to the pathologist per my oncologist's orders, and I was hospitalized. My Neutrophils (one of the components of your immune system) were zero. I was in isolation in the hospital for more than two days while they gave me intravenous immune support supplements. My friend managed my home while I recovered for my next round of chemotherapy and stayed until just before my next treatment. The worst part of the treatment with docetaxel was the enormous amounts of cortisone I had to take with it to minimize the side effects, causing major insomnia. *When I think of You as I lie on my bed, I meditate on You during the night watches because You are my helper; I will rejoice in the shadow of Your wings.* (Psalm 63:6-7 CSB)

My daughter from Australia and her youngest arrived shortly after my sixth treatment. Once again, I developed a fever and had to be hospitalized, but this time only overnight. Having my daughter and granddaughter with me for 12 days while I was recovering was such a blessing. God had sent two angels to look after me. The whole time I was also being carried by an army of prayer warriors. *Again, here is what I tell you. Suppose two of you on earth agree about anything you ask for. My Father in heaven will do it for you. Where two or three people gather in my name, I am there with them."* (Matthew 18:19-20 NIRV)

Only afterward did I learn that my husband had been worried that I would not make it, but God held me in His hand. *Yea, though I walk through the valley of the shadow of death, I will fear no evil; For You are with me; Your rod and Your staff, they comfort me.* (Psalm 23:4 NKJV)

The oncologist decided against the last two sessions of chemotherapy. I had returned to work and would not be able to miss every third Friday and perhaps be hospitalized on Monday and still be able to finish preparations for the student practical classes each week. Instead, I would undergo five weeks of daily radiation, which meant driving 20 minutes after my morning job, Monday to Friday, for the treatment. There was to be a slight pause before the radiation therapy would commence as my body had taken a good hammering. This treatment, together with the daily traveling, was very tiring, and the more treatments I had, the more tender the skin became. Clothes touching the position of radiation were very uncomfortable.

Three weeks after the treatment was completed, I ran/walked the Two Oceans half marathon with my son. I can witness that this happened only by the grace of God. *But those who trust in the Lord will receive new strength. They will fly as high as eagles. They will run and not get tired. They will walk and not grow weak.* (Isaiah 40:31 NIRV)

God added yet another blessing as we visited my daughter in Australia three months later, and she and I ran the Gold Coast half marathon together. It was so special to run with both my son and daughter in one year on two continents. I felt as though I was one of God's favorites—receiving so many blessings while going through this whole terrible AND wonderful journey.

I experienced first-hand the promise, *"For I know the plans I have for you,"* declares the Lord, *"plans to prosper you and not to harm you, plans to give you hope and a future."* (Jeremiah 29:11 NIV)

I pray that this journey of mine has assured you that we serve an awesome God who loves us more than we will ever understand. When we walk with Him, we can experience true JOY despite our circumstances.

> *Glorify the Lord with me; let us exalt His name together.* (Psalm 34:3 NIV)

Joy in Our Troubles & Afflictions

Finding joy when we are afflicted and walking through some of the hardest things in life can be incredibly challenging. How can we walk in joy and suffer at the same time? How can God allow afflictions to come our way and expect us to count it all joy? We must choose to expect God to bring us deep joy in all circumstances. You see, joy is not just a feeling. It is a God-produced emotion that comes from experiencing God's complete control of our lives.

When faced with troubles and challenges, we need to ask God to bring joy to our hearts amid suffering. And we can be assured that when we seek Him, He will show up! God is a personal God, and when you go to Him, He will gently grab your face and whisper to you, "My child, I see the end from the beginning. I knew this was going to happen before you were born. I've got you, and I will not leave you. You will see the beauty and joy that will come from this because you will help others through their journey as you walk through yours. Others will see Me in you, and you will walk with joy—a joy that only comes from Me. A joy that will bring others to know Me."

When we face challenges and troubles that come our way, God has a way of turning our mourning into joy. But we must choose to see the goodness of God in our afflictions. We must choose to see how God is moving in our lives, even in our suffering.

> *For you have been my help, and in the shadow of your wings I will sing for joy.* (Psalm 63:7 ESV)

God is our help, and He will never leave us. Although it may sometimes seem like He is not present or does not see the pain we are walking through, we must remember that He feels everything we feel. He *does* see you in your pain. And He desires to bring joy to your life. Even through our suffering, we can lean on the fact that joy and sorrow *can* dance together—just like a father and daughter dance on her wedding day, the swaying back and forth goes so beautifully together. Joy and sorrow can coexist in your life. Amid troubles and afflictions, joy can be present through God's strength. We just need to open our eyes to see the beauty of the dance—the beautiful dance God has given us of His love.

When you feel that you can no longer walk through the troubles and afflictions of life, press into Jesus, allowing Him to create a joy deep down inside you that will enable you to conquer what you are walking through. When we submit to God and allow Him to lead the dance, He will ensure that even through our troubles and afflictions, we will experience His beautiful and unspeakable joy.

Connie Ann VanHorn

Connie Ann VanHorn is an ambassador and best-selling author for Women World Leaders. She serves on the Leadership Team and is an ongoing featured writer for Voice of Truth magazine. Connie has a heart for encouraging all people to find their God-given purpose.

Connie is an ordinary person whom God spared and gave new life. She is passionate about sharing her story in hopes that God will use it to change lives. Connie wants the whole world to know about her amazing and loving God. She understands that we are all called to share in the same mission.

Connie resides in Winston-Salem, North Carolina, where she has participated in several discipleship classes and taught Sunday school to international students. She has also attended Bible classes at Vintage Bible College.

Being a mother is by far Connie's greatest accomplishment and her first, best ministry. She dreams of changing the world by sharing Jesus and raising world-changers who have a kingdom perspective.

She enjoys being active in her community, making bracelets, journaling, and spending most of her time with her family. Connie wants her readers to know that it's ok to be broken—it's in our broken place that we find God. See past messy, see past broken, and you might just see a miracle.

Broken Vessel

By Connie Ann VanHorn

Dear Tootles,
As it turns out
Life would be hard
Messy
We would fall a lot
Get back up
Fall again
We would struggle to let go
We would travel different roads
Sometimes alone
We would wander through the darkness
But chase down the light
As it turns out
You would get there before me
I bet it's beautiful
I'll see you again one day
Enjoy Home
Say hello from time to time
I'll sing to you like when we were kids
I'll cherish your letter always
I'll make sure they know your name
Love you always, Binks

Today was a hard day. I was having lunch at a restaurant when I got the worst call. My dad had been calling me frantically. I didn't realize that my phone was on silent. I had missed a call from my brothers as well. My stomach sank. My thoughts went immediately to my mom. In my entire adult life, I've never lost anyone this close to me. I was just saying weeks earlier that I'm not sure how I would react if someone close to me passed away.

I decided to return my dad's call while I was sitting in the restaurant. I held the phone to my ear, trembling a bit and hoping everything was ok. When my dad answered the phone, I could barely make out what he was saying.

"Amanda is dead." That's all I heard.

My entire body went numb, and I felt my heart pump as if it was on the outside of my body. I burst into tears, ran as fast as I could to the bathroom, and shut the door behind me. I slid my back down the wall to the ground, pulled my knees up to my chest, tucked my head, and cried.

Hundreds of miles away, my baby sister had died alone—broken and scared in her bed. And I wasn't there to help her.

When we were little girls, I had an over-the-top imagination, always dreaming of big things. At one point, I said I was going to be a country music star, and Amanda believed it. Amanda would spend hours listening to me sing. I can still see her sitting on the edge of the bed, looking up at me and saying, "Wow, you are going to be a star one day." She believed in me so much that I believed that I could sing. As it turns out, singing was not my calling. But the way she looked at me convinced made me I was great.

Amanda is just a couple of years younger than me. Born prematurely, she had educational and emotional delays and was very small for her age. She was the baby of the family and so sweet-natured. I never witnessed her being mean throughout our early childhood. Although she had every reason to be hateful and unkind, it just was not her spirit.

Our childhood was hard and traumatic, and we suffered greatly. Amanda suffered differently than I did. We spent a lot of time with my aunt, who was an angel in my eyes. She taught us about love and kindness and that you can still have joy in the worst circumstances. Her smile lights up in my memories. Aunt lived in the projects in Florida. Her house was extremely hot—with no air conditioning—and covered in roaches. But we didn't seem to mind at all. I slept alone on the couch with a fan blowing on me, which was wonderful. I felt loved and safe with Aunt.

My memories of this part of my childhood are very different from my sister. I have no memory of sexual abuse, even though I was right there with her. I escaped the horror that haunted Amanda for years. I witnessed and experienced my share of trauma, but this was unimaginable. I didn't know that Amanda was being sexually abused. I think I would have spoken out. Maybe I would have been scared.

Amanda struggled to find her place in this world. She couldn't find it at school. The educational delays and the peer pressure combined were just too much. I could barely survive it myself. Amanda struggled with emotional disabilities that were not diagnosed until she was an adult. She had bipolar disorder and social anxiety that was so extreme she never wanted to leave the house. She hated the way she looked and never felt pretty or confident.

Her story is similar to many people who come from trauma and abuse. She turned to all the wrong people and things to fill her empty places. She allowed people to take advantage of her, and some abused her greatly. She found her identity in negative groups that introduced her to drugs and alcohol. And unfortunately, alcohol abuse was a generational curse that had plagued my family for years.

My siblings and I came out of trauma with different struggles. For me, it was never drugs and alcohol. My battle became seeking love and acceptance while making sure I never let anyone close enough to hurt me. I coped by becoming a runner. When things got hard, that was my cue to exit. My sisters, haunted by their past, used everything and anything to cover their pain.

Amanda had one season of joy in her life, marked by her precious daughter, Madi Ann. I was honored when Madi was given my middle name. Amanda never thought she could have children, yet she desperately wanted to feel this kind of love. During this season, she was the happiest I've ever seen her. She was so excited to have a little girl but also scared to death. Her greatest fear was that she wouldn't know how to be a mom. Madi was the sweetest baby. I remember visiting Amanda after she had Madi and seeing this gigantic smile on Amanda's face. She knew she had just done something great. Amanda was able to fight off her demons for a few years. But then she moved back to Florida, and life became hard again. Whether it was her environment or being around old friends and memories, her demons came back into her life.

Amanda's addiction became the greatest fight of her life. I spent countless hours on the phone with my sister, listening to her cries to God. She wanted out of her addiction and the pain it was causing. She knew letting go meant she had to deal with herself, and she wasn't ready to do that. Her addiction grew to be more than drugs. She was now fighting alcoholism. She knew that this was not the life that her daughter deserved. She tried to keep Madi with her, but eventually, the state removed her from Amanda's care. Amanda wasn't strong enough to deal with this loss. It broke her even more, and she never recovered.

Amanda never wanted to lose Madi, and it crushed her daily. I truly believe that God knew Madi would be the greatest piece of Amanda's puzzle. God made it known that He had a plan for Madi's life. I tried to keep Madi in our family. She came to live with me in North Carolina the summer before she was adopted. This is one of the hardest moments in my life and a time I struggle to speak about. I felt that I failed Madi, but I have faith that our good God had a different plan for her. The short time Madi stayed with me was just a temporary stop for what He was preparing for her. We don't always understand God's ways or the pain left behind, but we can trust that His ways are better. A few months after Madi left with a piece of my heart, God revealed to me the reason she was here. It was a reason that had a purpose for my life and the precious little girl that would carry my middle name. We were connected in His plan for our lives. I trust Him.

We were told that Madi was adopted by a loving Christian family. Amanda knew that she couldn't give Madi the life she deserved. We spoke about Madi coming home one day and preparing her room with all the things she had saved for her. This gave Amanda great hope. Amanda kept a journal for Madi in anticipation of writing this story one day.

After Amanda passed, my dad gave me her Bible, the same Bible I had given her almost three years before the day of her passing. She had marked up pages and underlined scripture. Amanda was reading her Bible, keeping it close by. She had the words "Broken Vessel" written on the cover page. We had spent time on the phone talking about God and how Amanda was going to get better and help people one day. She cried out to God. She wanted to share her story, and she wanted her life to count. She wanted others to know that brokenness can be purposeful and that He can turn ashes into something beautiful. Madi will be a part of that something beautiful that came out of Amanda's life.

And we know that in all things God works for the good of those who love Him, who have been called according to His purpose. (Romans 8:28 NIV)

Finding *Joy Unspeakable* at a funeral:

I was asked to share a message at Amanda's funeral. The pastor had invited me to give the opening and closing messages. I was scared to death. I didn't know if I would be able to hold it together. I was also afraid of public speaking, but I knew I needed to do this for Amanda. The day before I left for Florida to attend the funeral, I found a letter that Amanda had written me years prior. I wasn't looking for this letter, and I found it in the most random place. I had no idea the letter existed. In it, Amanda reminded me of my worth and that she always believed in me. She told me not to be afraid, and she wrote so many other powerful statements. This letter gave me courage. She found a way to speak to me from heaven.

On the day of the funeral, I stood in front of everyone and shared about Amanda. I also shared God's redeeming love and hope in Jesus. The pastor and I decided we would use Amanda's celebration of life to celebrate Jesus' love. We invited others to know this amazing love. We prayed that if anyone needed to surrender or be saved, this would be the day. In the hope that others might be encouraged to make a change for themselves, at the service I shared how I gave my heart to Jesus, was transformed, and became a new creation in August 2014.

> *Therefore, if anyone is in Christ, the new creation has come: The old has gone, the new is here!* (2 Corinthians 5:17 NIV)

God wants all His children to come to Him. He wants you just the way you are and right where you are. He will walk through all the hard things with us. God doesn't look at our past or the struggles we face today—He looks at our hearts. I boldly proclaimed that we don't have to walk alone—tired and worn. If we long to hold hands with the One who created us, today is the day to reach our arms out to Him.

That is the same way I surrendered my heart. I repented to Jesus in my prayers and asked Him to come into my heart and guide me. I truly believe that Jesus died for me. He loved me from the very beginning, and He patiently waited for me to realize that I couldn't do life alone. He climbed up on that cross for me. I know that I can't get to heaven without Him, and heaven is where I long to be.

> *If you declare with your mouth, "Jesus is Lord," and believe in your heart that God raised Him from the dead, you will be saved.* (Romans 10:9 NIV)

I was able to share all this at Amanda's funeral without fear. I stood in front of everyone with more courage than I'd had my entire adult life. It was the same courage I had when I would sing to Amanda when we were younger. I wasn't afraid or filled with self-doubt. She was with me and everyone in the room. We all felt it.

Amanda's favorite color was purple, and the entire room was dripping in purple. Some guests arrived wearing purple, not knowing it was her favorite color, and all of her guests were handed a purple ribbon upon arrival. The ribbon represented addiction awareness and, ironically, her favorite color. I had invited several friends to attend. The one special woman who showed up to support me was wearing a purple bracelet that I had gifted her weeks before Amanda's passing.

We all witnessed many miracles on this day. Several people surrendered their burdens at the altar, and one life got saved. Amanda used to tell me, "If one life is changed by my life, then I guess it counted."

It counted. It counted for the kingdom of heaven. And it will continue to count until the work is finished.

Amanda was a broken vessel for God's work. Never count yourself out or think that you are too broken. God can use a broken vessel.

> *But we have this treasure in jars of clay, to show that the surpassing power belongs to God and not to us.* (2 Corinthians 4:7 ESV)

The takeaway:

This race. This life.
It's growing us towards death that leads us home.
With Jesus.
Heaven is our home.
This is our hope.

We are going to suffer. It's part of it.
Suffering changes us.
Pain can be our best teacher.
Don't give up!

God has a plan, and He is walking through it with you.
I couldn't see the light at the end of my suffering.
It was scary and painful, but we learn to be the flashlight walking through dark places.

Keep moving. Believe in God's miracles.
God knows what it takes to get glory out of your life.
We grow in our suffering and brokenness.

This race. This life.
Sometimes it's messy, not very pretty, painful, and just hurts really bad.
But...
If we can persevere and get back up. Go at it again...
Allow God to work.
It's perfection.
It's beautiful.
It's leading us
and others through us,
Home!

It's a miracle.

Be thankful for scars and broken pots.
It's our scars that tell of who He is in our lives and the courage we
have built within us to get back up.
Keep going!

Come as you are. Give this race your best. And daydream about the day we stand face to face with Jesus, and He looks at you and says,

"Welcome Home."

Amanda lost her earthly life to an accidental overdose. She didn't want to die. I'm assuming she knew the risk involved. But Amanda thought she was invincible and her addiction was greater than those fears. Her autopsy report reads that she died from a lethal dose of fentanyl. Fentanyl is labeled the most dangerous drug in America and is unlike any other drug problem in modern history—far beyond a traditional drug epidemic. And unfortunately, the crisis is likely to get worse. We need to educate young people and offer more resources to the public. If you or someone you know is struggling with addiction, there is hope. Please contact your church or local substance abuse hotline for help.

We can find hope in Jesus. We don't have to be prisoners of our pain or our past—Jesus can release us. We have the choice to partner with God and see ourselves as we are in heaven: whole and made perfect. God is greater than anything we face on earth.

> *You, dear children, are from God and have overcome them, because the One who is in you is greater than the one who is in the world.* (1 John 4:4 NIV)

I hope Amanda's story has shone a light on the importance of each life—including yours. God can use everything for good and the eternal weight of glory. Never lose heart.

Your struggle isn't meaningless. Even when you can't see what it's doing, you can trust that God is in control and He is greater than any force that can come against us. And when we focus on the glory of God, we can be certain He will infuse us with joy beyond the world's understanding.

I love you.

Amanda M. "Tootles" VanHorn
6/26/83 - 6/17/22
Always, "Binks"

Count It All Joy

> *Count it all joy, my brethren, when you meet various trials, for you know that the testing of your faith produces steadfastness. And let steadfastness have its full effect, that you may be perfect and complete, lacking in nothing.* (James 1:2-4 RSV)

Joy does not come naturally, even for Christians, especially during difficult times. We tend to worry and stress over situations and circumstances, which steals our peace and joy. Therefore, we have to make a conscious effort to choose joy in everything.

The Bible instructs us to rejoice in the midst of all things, even hardships. *Always be joyful because you belong to the Lord. I will say it again. Be joyful!* (Philippians 4:4 NIRV)

Joy does not mean you are ignoring or denying the pain or your circumstances, pretending to be happy, or having a positive attitude no matter what. Instead, joy is knowing that "something" far greater outweighs the bad, and that "something" is incomparable! *I consider that our present sufferings are not worth comparing with the glory that will be revealed in us.* (Romans 8:18 NIV)

So, what is that "something"?

The foremost reason for joy in the life of a believer is salvation! You have been saved from the condemnation and wrath of God. (Romans 5:8-11) As a Christ-follower, you have the assurance of having been saved to eternal life, your name is recorded in heaven, and you belong to God's kingdom!

Joy comes in an inner confidence that reminds you that tough times and pain will not last forever; there is light at the end of the tunnel (and it's not a speeding train coming at you!) There is a rainbow after the rain. Having faith allows us to take a stand, to endure just about anything, even death, recognizing that "something" much better is coming! *For our light and momentary troubles are achieving for us an eternal glory that far outweighs them all.* (2 Corinthians 4:17 NIV)

A Christian's joy also comes from Christ in us—the hope of glory! (Colossians 1:27) God infuses us with unexplainable joy when He resides in us. True joy is simply not possible without Jesus. We can unashamedly cling to the gift of salvation, knowing it can never be destroyed or taken away; it won't spoil or fade. Once we accept Jesus Christ as our Savior, joy is ours forever. This is *Joy Unspeakable!*

Peter says it well:

> *Praise be to the God and Father of our Lord Jesus Christ! In his great mercy he has given us new birth into a living hope through the resurrection of Jesus Christ from the dead, and into an inheritance that can never perish, spoil or fade. This inheritance is kept in heaven for you, who through faith are shielded by God's power until the coming of the salvation that is ready to be revealed in the last time. In all this you greatly rejoice, though now for a little while you may have had to suffer grief in all kinds*

> *of trials. These have come so that the proven genuineness of your faith—of greater worth than gold, which perishes even though refined by fire—may result in praise, glory and honor when Jesus Christ is revealed. Though you have not seen him, you love him; and even though you do not see him now, you believe in him and are filled with an inexpressible and glorious joy, for you are receiving the end result of your faith, the salvation of your souls.* (1 Peter 1:3-9 NIV)

Joy is ours to choose! And when we do, God turns our miseries into ministries. Yes, you can have joy amid hardship and trials. Claim it! Carry it with you! And never let it go!

> *Rejoice always, pray continually, give thanks in all circumstances, for this is God's will for you in Christ Jesus.* (1 Thessalonians 5:16-18 NIV)

Afterword

The best test of joy is in the valleys of our lives. The ability to be joyful in all things is a measure of our faith. You may not be able to see God's hand while you are going through trials and hardships, but you can rejoice in knowing you can trust His heart to do what is best for your situation. He will never leave you nor forsake you. He is rarely early but never late in coming to the rescue. You can depend on Him who is able to do exceedingly and abundantly more than you could ever imagine.

Because of His promises, you can count it all joy! When?

- When you feel like you do not matter, be overjoyed because there is One who sees into the depths of your soul.

- When you feel the storm is too strong, rejoice that there is One who will calm it with His voice.

- When you cannot see in front of you, feel joy in that there is One carrying you.

- When you are broken, be joyful that there is One who puts you back together.

- When you are hurt to the core, you can still have joy because there is One who heals, expecting nothing in return.

- When you feel hopeless, embrace indescribable joy from the One who gives you perfect peace.

- When you cannot speak, you can have joy deep in your heart from the One who hears you through your tears.

- When you see the darkness all around, see joy at the end of the tunnel because there is One whose light is so much brighter.

- When you have little faith, jump for joy; there is One who says just a mustard seed of faith is all you need.

- When the ashes are on the ground, you can still experience undefeatable joy; there is One that picks them up and creates a masterpiece.

- When there is doubt, joy is supernatural from the One who brings clarity through His Spirit.

- When you want to wallow in your shame, praise Him and sing with joy; He is the One who calls you to worship because He loves you.

- When you want to be accepted, shout with joy that there is One who has chosen you and called you by name.

- When there is a winding road of uncertainty, walk it in joy; there is One who will make the path straight with His hand.

- When you don't want to walk by yourself through the trial, hold hands with joy, the One that has never left you.

- When you feel your sin is too great, count it all joy that there is One whose redemption covers you from head to toe.

- When you fully surrender your life, JESUS is the One who has been waiting for you the whole time. His love, mercy, and grace far surpass all you need. He sees you, He knows you, He adores you, He accepts you, and He is enough for you.

> *But He said to me, "My grace is sufficient for you, for my power is made perfect in weakness."* (2 Corinthians 12:9 NIV)

As you've read this book, please know that the authors have prayed for you. They have prayed you would recognize that true joy only comes from a relationship with Jesus Christ. We have prayed you would encounter the joy and peace that passes all human understanding in all your circumstances. We have prayed that joy will ooze out of you in every situation as your testimony of the One who lives in you, *because the One who is in you is greater than the one who is in the world.* (1 John 4:4 NIV) And we have prayed that you have and will experience and praise God for *Joy Unspeakable: Regardless of Your Circumstances.*

May you trust God through the saving blood of Jesus Christ and seek Him by faith for Joy Unspeakable in your life.

> *May the God of hope fill you with all joy and peace as you trust in Him, so that you may overflow with hope by the power of the Holy Spirit.* (Romans 15:13 NIV)

More from WPP!

World Publishing and Productions (WPP) was birthed in obedience to God's call. Our mission is to empower writers to walk in their God-given purpose as they share their God story with the world. We offer one-on-one coaching and a complete publishing experience. To find out more about how we can help you become a published author or to purchase books written to share God's glory, please visit: www.worldpublishingandproductions.com

Surrendered: Yielded With Purpose will help you recognize with awe that surrendering to God is far more effective than striving alone. When we let go of our own attempts to earn God's favor and rely on Jesus Christ, we receive a deeper intimacy with Him and a greater power to serve Him.

United Men of Honor: Overcoming Adversity Through Faith will help you armor up, become fit to fight, and move forward with what it takes to be an honorable leader. Over twenty authors in this book share their accounts of God's provision, care, and power as they proclaim His Word.

Embrace the Journey: Your Path to Spiritual Growth will strengthen and empower you to step boldly in faith. These stories, along with expertly placed expositional teachings will remind you that no matter what we encounter, we can always look to God, trusting HIS provision, strength, and direction.

Victories: Claiming Freedom in Christ presents expository teaching coupled with individual stories that testify to battles conquered victoriously through the power of Jesus Christ. The words in this book will motivate and inspire you and give you hope as God awakens you to your victory!

World Publishing and Productions

Empowering you to share your God-given story with the world.

Made in the USA
Middletown, DE
30 April 2023